URDU

FOR

BEGINNERS

KHAWAJA MUHAMMAD ZAKARIYA

Library of Congress Cataloging in Publication Data

Zakariya, Khawaja Muhammad
        Urdu for Beginners.
        1. Urdu 2. Language learning I. Title II. Author
ISBN: 1-871031-02-8

CONTENTS

Transliteration Scheme 9

1. Chapter I   URDU SCRIPT   11

2. Chapter II   GRAMMAR... 22

3. Chapter III GENDERS AND NUMBERS 32

4. Chapter IV   TENSES   37

5. Chapter V   SOME MORE GRAMMAR 64

   EXERCISES.. 80

PREFACE

Dr. Kh. Muhammad Zakariya is Professor & Chairman of Urdu Department, Punjab University, Lahore. Dr. Zakariya has written "Urdu for Beginners" and "Key to Urdu for Beginners" on our request.

The book together with its key is being published by National Language Authority, Islamabad.

The author has tought Urdu to foreigners at the Oriental College, Lahore. This experience has certainly helped him much to write a short but comprehensive book for the beginners of Urdu learners.

The book is based on five chapters, discussing characteristics of Urdu script, Urdu alphabet and its English equivalent, Urdu letters & their shape groups, Transliteration-Scheme, parts of speech etc. In the last chapter of the book the author has given exercises for reading practice. Dialogues and simple essays on various topics have been included in these exercises.

Dr. Zakariya has used simple & limited vocabulary of everyday conversation in this book, thus making it more easy, interesting and useful for the biginners of Urdu learners.

I have every hope that "Urdu for Beginners" will prove useful for foreigners as well as the native beginners having English as their medium of instruction striving to learn Urdu as a language.

Dr. Jameel Jalibi

INTRODUCTION

The reason for writing this book is that I was appointed to teach Urdu to foreigners at the Oriental College, Lahore some twenty five years ago. The idea of elaborating the notes taken at that time into a book seized my mind since then, but it took me twenty five long years to translate the idea into action. Thank God, the book is in the hands of readers.

The book is short, precise, to the point and written in a non technical language, as far as possible. The matter has been arranged systematically. The vocabulary used in the book is useful for everyday conversation. It is written on the style of a "teach yourself" book, but no book on the subject can really serve the purpose of "teach yourself" in itself, for it is not possible to learn the pronunciation of letters and words without the help of a teacher. The learner is, therefore, advised not to depend entirely on the 'Romanised Version' of Urdu script, as no system of transliteration (except, perhaps, that of International Phonetic Association – abbreviated as IPA) can do justice to the phonetics of a language. The portion of grammar, however, can be learnt without the help of a teacher, as it is mainly descriptive in nature.

I have restricted the scope of the book to a very small vocabulary – three hundred words in all – so that the learner may comfortably master it. Once he gets familiar with the structure of Urdu grammar, he may gradually enrich his vocabulary through his personal efforts. To provide him this opportunity, and also to make him familiar with the current idiom of Urdu language, a full chapter, exercises for reading practice, has been appended to the book.

Kh. Muhammad Zakariya
Professor and Chairman
Department of Urdu
University of the Punjab
Lahore, Pakistan

TRANSLITERATION SCHEME

The following scheme of transliteration has been adopted in this book.

Vowels

a	is to be pronounced like				*u* in cut.
á	"	"	"	"	*a* in father.
ā	"	"	"	"	*a* in bat.
ē	"	"	"	"	*e* in prey.
ee	"	"	"	"	*ee* in teeth.
i	"	"	"	"	*i* in sit.
o	"	"	"	"	*o* in gold.
au	"	"	"	"	*o* in pot.
u	"	"	"	"	*u* in put.
oo	"	"	"	"	*oo* in boot.
e	"	"	"	"	*e* in pen.
y	"	"	"	"	*y* in yesterday.
ei	"	"	"	"	*i* in tiger.

Note: Nasal 'n' is to be indicated by putting a small curve over "n" like "ñ".

Consonants

1. b, d, f, j, l, m, n, p, s, t and z:
    to be pronounced like their English sounds.
2. ḍ and ṭ:
    Softer than the English d and t sounds.
    Resemble French d and t.
3. g:
    Like the sound of 'g' in 'gun' and not like 'gem'.
4. h:
    To be pronounced like 'h' in 'huge'.

5. q:
Rather heavy and guttural sound as in 'quarter'.

6. r:
An aspirated sound like 'r' in rod but not a suppressed sound like 'car'.

7. ṛ:
Heavier and harder sound than 'r'. While pronouncing it the tip of the tongue should touch the palate (roof of the mouth).

8. ṛh:
Still more heavy and hard sound than 'ṛ'.

9. bh, dh, jh, kh, gh, ph and th:
Heavier and aspirated forms of b, d, j, k, g, p and t sounds respectively.

10. ḍh and ṭh:
Heavier and aspirated forms of ḍ and ṭ sounds.

11. k̲:
Guttural sound, resembling German 'r'.

12. g:
Guttural sound, with no equivalent sound in English.

13.
Sound like long á, but to be pronounced in the throat.

14. ch and sh:
Sound like 'ch' in Church and 'sh' in share, respectively.

15. c̲h:
Heavier and aspirated form of 'ch' sound.

16. zh:
Sounds like 'z' in 'azure'.

Note: There are four letters for the English 'z' in Urdu – ‏ز‏ ، ‏ذ‏ ، ‏ژ‏ ، ‏ض‏ – and three for 's' – ‏ث‏ ، ‏س‏ ، ‏ص‏ – but since their pronunciation is similar, therefore, there is no need of transliterating them differently.

Chapter I

SCRIPT

I
Urdu Script

The Urdu script is an adaptation from the Arabic script, the notable features of which are as under:

1. Horizontally it is written from right to left and vertically, upside down.

2. Most of the letters are connectible with one another on either side, but some of them can only be joined to the preceding and not the succeeding letter.

3. These letters are divisible into fifteen distinct "shape-groups". The letters falling in a shape group might radically differ in sound from one another but are distinguishable by the 'signs' and 'dots' placed above or below each letter.

4. While forming words, most of the letters retain only a part of their full shapes, but are still recognisable because of the number of dots and other signs, which remain intact and serve as a guide to the learner in identifying them.

5. The lerner should, first try to acquaint himself with the full shape of each letter before proceeding any further.

II
Urdu Alphabet and its English Equivalents

Urdu letter	Pronunciation	English Equivalent
آ	It is a long vowel like 'a' in "father".	*a*

11

	(alif)	Short vowel like 'u' in "cut" if it occurs in the beginning of a word; but it is always a long vowel if it comes in the middle or at the end of a word.	
ب	(bē)	Like 'b' in English, but less aspirated	b
پ	(pē)	Like 'p'; less aspirated	p
ت	(tē)	Like French 't'; softer than English 't'	t
ٹ	(tē)	Like English 't' but less aspirated	t
ث	(sē)	In Urdu, unlike Arabic, it sounds like English 's'	s
ج	(jeem)	English 'j' sound but less aspirated	j
چ	(chē)	Like English 'ch' sound as in "Church"	ch
ح	(hē)	English 'h' sound as in "hen"	h
خ	(khē)	Resembles French 'r'; guttural sound; it has no exact equivalent in English.	
د	(dāl)	Like 'd' in French. Similar to the sound of 'th' in the article "the".	d
ڈ	(dāl)	Like 'd' in English	d
ذ	(zāl)	Like 'z' sound in English	z
ر	(rē)	Like 'r' sound in 'rose', but to be pronounced more clearly.	r
ڑ	(rē)	Like 'r' sound in English but harder.	r
ز	(zē)	Also English 'z' sound like zāl " ذ "	z
ژ	(zhē)	Heavier and aspirated sound of "z" as in "azure"	zh
س س س	(seen)	Sounds like 's' in 'sun'	s
ش ش ش	(sheen)	Similar to English 'sh' sound in "shine"	sh

12

ص	(suād)	Another letter for 's' sound	s
ض	(zuād)	Yet another letter for 'z' sound	z
ط	(toē)	Another letter having soft 't' sound	t
ظ	(zoē)	'z' sound	z
ع	(an)	Like long 'a' sound in "father" but to be pronounced in the throat.	
غ	(gan)	It has no equivalent in English. It is a guttural sound having some similarity to 'gh' sound in English.	
ف	(fē)	Like 'f' in "fan".	f
ق	(qāf)	Like 'q' sound in 'quarrel', but to be pronounced in the throat.	q
ک	(kāf)	Like 'k' sound in 'kite'	k
گ	(gāf)	Like 'g' sound in 'gun'	g
ل	(lām)	Like 'l' sound in English	l
م	(meem)	Like 'm' sound in English	m
ن	(noon)	Like 'n' sound in English	n
و	(wāo)	Like 'v' sound in English	v
ه	(hē)	Another letter for 'h' sound	h
ی	(yē)	Sounds like 'ee' as in 'tree'	ee
ے	(yē)	Sounds like 'ai' as in 'paid'	ai

We have seen above that some letters are similar in sound but despite this similarity they are not interchangeable in writing; for example ' ص ' cannot take the place of ' س ', and ' ط ' cannot be changed for ' ض ' or ' ت ' and so on. Therefore, each word has to be learnt along with its fixed spelling.

III
Vowels

Urdu speaking people use twelve vowels in their everyday speech. Only six of them are used in writing. Some list ' ء ' (hamza) as another vowel. It resembles 'y' sound in 'cycle'. Vowels are short as well as long. Short vowels are ‿ (zabar), ‿ (pēsh) and ‿ (zēr) which are the abbreviated forms of (alif), (wāo) and ى (yē), respectively. Vowel diacritics are seldom printed in books excepting those written for beginners. The remaining vowels are pronounced by the reader, but are not expressed in the symbols. However, to avoid difficulties in transliteration, the author of the Urdu books for foreign students, generally adopt same system for expressing these sounds in symbols. A system of transliteration, therefore, has been adopted in this book as well, keeping in mind the students who are interested in learning Urdu conversation and not the script.

IV

Shape Groups of Letters

Urdu alphabet is divisible into fifteen distinct shape groups. The group wise list of these letters is as under:

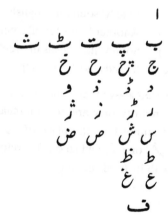

14

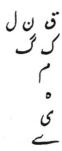

The learner should grasp the the structure of each letter along with its distinguishing marks. This will help him not only in identifying each individual letter but also the shape-group in which it falls.

V

Consonants

Some consonants are aspirated and some unaspirated. The former are pronounced with full breath and the latter with a half-breath. Those pronounced with a half breath are eleven in number:

ب پ ت ٹ ج چ ڈ ڈ ڑ ک گ

When it is intended to pronounce these consonants with a full breath, the letter 'h' is suffixed to them. Thus 'b' becomes 'bh' and 'p' becomes 'ph'.

In Urdu script a peculiar form of 'h' (ھ) is suffixed to these letters, known as "do chashmi hē" (which means 'h' with two eyes), for its shape looks like two eyes joined together.

The strongly aspirated forms of the letters mentioned above are as under:

15

The aspirated forms of l, m and n are as under:

ھ - مھ - لھ

however, they are seldom used.

VI

Initial, medial and final forms

While   words from the individual letters, each letter undergoes slight change in its original full form. These changes which are applicable to a majority of letters, assume three forms – initial, medial and final – detailed below:

full form	initial	medial	final
ب	ﺑ	ﺒ	ﺐ
پ	ﭘ	ﭙ	ﭗ
ت	ﺗ	ﺘ	ﺖ
ٹ	ﭨ	ﭩ	ﭧ
ث	ﺛ	ﺜ	ﺚ
ج	ﺟ	ﺠ	ﺞ
چ	ﭼ	ﭽ	ﭻ
ح	ﺣ	ﺤ	ﺢ
خ	ﺧ	ﺨ	ﺦ
س	ﺳ	ﺴ	ﺲ
ش	ﺷ	ﺸ	ﺶ
ص	ﺻ	ﺼ	ﺺ
ض	ﺿ	ﻀ	ﺾ
ط	ﻃ	ﻄ	ﻂ
ظ	ﻇ	ﻈ	ﻆ

16

ع	ﻊ	ﻌ	ﻋ
غ	ﻎ	ﻐ	ﻏ
ف	ﻒ	ﻔ	ﻓ
ق	ﻖ	ﻘ	ﻗ
ک	ﮏ	ﮑ	ﮐ
گ	ﮓ	ﮕ	ﮔ
ل	ﻞ	ﻠ	ﻟ
م	ﻢ	ﻤ	ﻣ
ن	ﻦ	ﻨ	ﻧ
ہ	ﮦ	ﮨ	ﮩ
ی	ﻰ	ﻴ	ﻳ
ے	ﻲ	ﻲ	ﮯ

The following letters are non-connectors, therefore, they do not undergo change of initial or medial sort.

$$ا$$
$$د \quad ڈ \quad ذ$$
$$ر \quad ڑ \quad ز \quad ژ$$
$$و$$

They can be joined only to the preceding and not to the succeeding letter, therefore, they assume only the final form of change in the following manner:

17

Reading Drill-I

Non-connector words

دا   را   آ   وا   زا   ذا

دال   رام   آم   وار   زار   ذات

رات   راگ   دام   راج   راز

روز   روم   روک   روگ

Combinations of connector and non-connector words

بابا   پاپا   تابا   آٹا   پایا

تالا   لایا   کھایا   سویا   رویا

Gained words

نہر   سر   شہر   کرم   گھر

جب   تب   شب   کب   تب

پیچ   بچ   بچ   بس   خس

وسن   مرین   بک   مرن   دل پل

ہم   خط   بھن   مچن   پل مل

مرنب   ٹب   جٹر   سٹھ   تن

تو   مو   رو   دن   لو

بن   پن   بو   سو   شب

یتم   گم   گن   گن   بت

دھل   گھر   دل   دن   بچل

پھر   پھل

18

Examples of three lettered words with long vowels

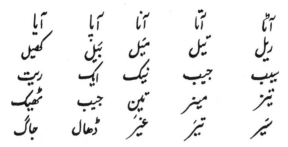

Examples of three lettered words with short vowels

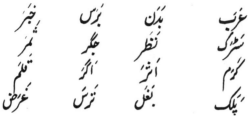

VIII
Amputation

When there is no short vowel between two consonants, it is indicated by the sign " ٘ ", called "jazm" placed in between the two consonants, as shown in the following examples:

(farsh)	فَرْش	(murgh)	مُرْغ
(jism)	جِسْم	(ilm)	عِلْم
(sabz)	سَبْز	(garm)	گَرْم

IX
Using a letter twice in a pair

There are many words in English in which a letter occurs twice in a pair, for example, in follow (double "l") and professor (double "s"). In Urdu also many words are formed like this, but in writing instead of doubling the letter a sign " ّ " called 'tashdeed' is placed on the top of the doubled letter, as illustrated below:

19

(abbá)	اَبّا	(kuttá)	کُتّا
(bachchá)	بچّہ	(sachchá)	سچّا
(bachchi)	بچّی	(batti)	بتّی

Note: In Urdu a doubled letter is pronounced more distinctly than in English.

Some verbs, in their infinitive forms are exceptions to this rule. The letter 'n' (ن) in such verbs is written twice instead of placing the sign of 'tashdeed' on the top of it. For example:

گننا   سُننا   چُننا   بننا

X

Nasal 'N' (ن)

When the nasal 'N' occurs at the end of a word it is written without a dot.

Examples:

ماں   کہاں   یہاں   مَیں   ہیں

But when it occurs in between, the sign " ٘ " is placed on the top of the letter, as in the following examples:

جنگ   رنگ   پانچ   آنکھ

XI

Reading Drill -II

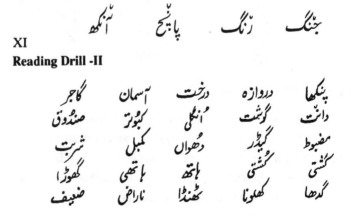

پنکھا	دروازہ	درخت	آسمان	گاجر
دانت	گوشت	اُنگلی	کبوتر	صندوق
مضبوط	گیدڑ	دھواں	کمبل	شربت
کشتی	کُشتی	ہاتھ	باتھی	گھوڑا
گدھا	کھلونا	ٹھنڈا	ناراض	ضعیف

طوطا قرآن لائن لاغر لکھی

قسمت جماعت قابل کوشش شخص

استاد ورزِش بھائی سینگ زنگ

شیشہ آہستہ چولھا ینخفا اچھا

گنواں دنیا عزیز تشریح ضمیر

شریف شریک پتنگ عظمت حفاظت

کہانی نشانی قمیجسی گاڑی لکڑی

استقبال زندگی آدمی آخری

حرکت خالی خاکی ترقی پچراسی

ثبوت پھونک عنقریب ملازمت پولیس

شعاع شغل شعور معقول مغلوب

نوراً نقریباً عمداً مثلاً عادتاً

خود خوش خواب خودی خواجہ

The examples of the words given in the last but one line are of pure Arabic origin. Whenever two small parallel lines are placed on the top of the last letter of an Arabic word (ًـ), it is to be pronounced like 'n' (ن).

In the last line ' و ' is silent. It is so because it occurs after "خ". In all such cases ' و ' is supposed to be silent.

21

Chapter II

GRAMMAR

I

Articles

The; A and An:

In English 'a' and 'an' are indefinite articles, whereas 'the' is a definite article. There is no equivalent of 'the' in Urdu. Similarly 'a' and 'an' are not used as articles in Urdu. 'A' is used in the sense of 'one' *i.e.*, numeral adjective only.

The following examples show the difference between the two languages on this point:

		English	*Transliteration*	*Urdu script*
(a)	1.	A man	Ádmi	آدمی
	2.	A woman	Áurat	عورت
	3.	A boy	Larká	لڑکا
	4.	An egg	Anda	انڈا
	5.	An arm	Bázoo	بازو
(b)	1.	The man	Ádmi	آدمی
	2.	The Woman	Áurat	عورت
	3.	The boy	Larká	لڑکا
	4.	The egg	Aṅda	انڈا
	5.	The arm	Bázoo	بازو

II

Demonstrative Pronouns

'This' is yēh (یہ) and 'that' is woh (وہ) in Urdu; as illustrated below:

(a)	1.	This man	yēh ádmi	یہ آدمی
	2.	This woman	yēh áurat	یہ عورت
(b)	1.	That house	woh makán	وہ مکان
	2.	That door	woh darwázá	وہ دروازہ

III
Possessive Pronouns

The following are some of the possessive pronouns used in English:

My, our, your, his and her.

They are used with nouns immediately following them as in the examples given below:

(a) my book, (b) our school, (c) your pen, (d) his house and (e) her watch

In English, the same possessive pronouns are used both for males and females in the first person (my, our) and second person (your), but in the third person 'his' is used for males and 'her' for females. In Urdu, on the contrary, different possessive pronouns are used for males and females in all the three persons, as is shown in the following table:

	English	Male		Female	
			Urdu		
1.	My	mērá	میرا	mēri	میری
2.	Your	tumhárá	تمہارا	tumhári	تمہاری
		ápká	آپ کا	ápki	آپ کی
3.	Our	hamárá	ہمارا	hamári	ہماری
4.	His/Her	uská	اس کا	uski	اس کی
5.	Their	unká	ان کا	unki	ان کی

Note: 'ápká' and 'ápki' for 'your' is a polite form of 'tumhárá' and 'tumhári' which can be used both for singulars and plurals.

Please remember that in Urdu all nouns, living or non living, are either males or females. For example, makán, pen, kutta and school are males but ghari pencil and gári are females. Male possessive pronouns end in á (1) and females end in 'i' (ی). In Urdu, like Enlgish, the possessive pronouns are used with nouns following them immediately.

23

Examples

	English	Urdu	
1.	My house	mērá makán	میرامکان
2.	My watch	meri ghaṛi	میری گھڑی
3.	Your pen	ṭumhárá qalam	تمہارا قلم
4.	Your dog	ápká kuttá	آپ کا کتّا
5.	Your pencil	ṭumhari pencil	تمہاری پنسل
6.	Your pencil	ápki pencil	آپ کی پنسل
7.	Our school	hamárá sakool	ہمارا سکول
8.	Our car	hamári gáṛi	ہماری گاڑی

In Urdu, unlike English, the noun preceding the possessive pronoun governs the pronoun. It is so in French as well.

Examples

	English	Urdu
1.	His watch	uskighaṛi(not uská gaṛi)
2.	Her pen	uská qalam (not uski qalam)

Note: Apka (آپ کا) and apki (آپ کی) are used out of respect, in place of tumhárá (تمہارا) and tumhári (تمہاری).

IV

Prepositions (Post Positions)

In English, a preposition always precedes a noun or pronoun and that is why it is called a pre-position; but in Urdu, on the contrary, it succeeds a noun or a pronoun and hence it is called post-position.

Here are some examples of English prepositions and their corresponding post-positions in Urdu.

24

English Prepositions	Urdu Postpositions	
1. From	sē	ـے
2. To	ko	کو
3. In	mēň	میں
4. On/At	par	پر
5. Upto	tak	یک

The following examples show the use of post-positions in Urdu:

Urdu		English Translation
1. kitáb sē	کتاب سے	from the book
2. Karachi ko	کراچی کو	to Karachi
3. páni mēň	پانی میں	in the water
4. mez par	میز پر	on the table
5. school tak	سکول یک	upto the school

Compound Postpositions

A compound post-position is made by prefixing kē (کے) or ki (کی) to a simple post-position.

examples

(a) Compound postpositions made by prefixing 'kē' (کے)

Urdu		English
1. kē pás	کے پاس	near
2. kē neechē	کے نیچے	under/below
3. kē peechē	کے پیچھے	behind
4. kē ágē	کے آگے	in front/before
5. kē sámnē	کے سامنے	in front/before
6. kē sáth	کے ساتھ	with
7. kē aňdar	کے اندر	inside
8. kē báhar	کے باہر	outside
9. kē wástē	کے واسطے	for
10. kē liyē	کے لیے	for

25

(b)   Compound postpositions made by prefixing 'ki' (کی)

	Urdu		English
1.	ki taraf	کی طرف	towards
2.	ki khátir	کی خاطر	for the sake of

V

Personal Pronouns

The following personal pronouns are used in place of subjects, in Urdu:

First Person	Urdu		English
Singular:	máň	میں	I
Plural:	ham	ہم	we
Second Person			
Singular:	too	تُو	thou
Plural:	tum	تُم	you
	áp	آپ	you (polite form)
Third Person			
Singular:	woh	وہ	he/she
Plural:	woh	وہ	they

In Urdu, as in English, the same pronouns are used both for males and females, in the first and second persons. However, in Urdu, the form of the verb tells us the gender of the pronoun, it refers to. As regards the third person, different pronouns are used for males and females in English, but this difference is confined to singular number only. In Urdu, on the contrary, the same pronoun is used both for males and females, in the third person also, as in the first and second persons, with the form of the verb indicating the gender of the pronoun it refers to.

Áp (آپ) is used as an honorific, both for one and more than one persons, in the second person.

26

VI

Conjugation of the verb "Honá" (ہونا)

In Urdu, all infinitives end in "ná" (نا). In English they are preceded by 'to'. "Honá" (ہونا), which means "to be" in English, is an important infinitive in Urdu. It is necessary to learn its conjugation, for we cannot make even simple sentences, without its proper knowledge.

Various inflections of the infinitive 'honá' (ہونا) are as under:

Subject		English	Urdu	
First Person				
Singular:		I am	mãñ hooñ	میں ہوں
Plural:		we are	ham hãñ	ہم ہیں
Second Person				
Singular:		thou art	too hā	تو ہے
Plural:		you are	tum ho	تم ہو
		ap hãñ	ap hãñ	آپ ہیں
Third Person				
Singular	(male)	he is	woh hā	وہ ہے
	(female)	she is	woh hā	وہ ہے
Plural	(male)	they are	woh hãñ	وہ ہیں
	(female)	they are	woh hãñ	وہ ہیں

VII

Making Sentences

In Urdu sentences, subject comes first. It is followed by the object. The verb comes at the end of the sentence. The following examples illustrate this point:

Urdu		English
1.	yeh kitab hā	یہ کتاب ہے	This is a book.
2.	woh mēz hā	وہ میز ہے	That is a table.
3.	yēh larkā hā	یہ لڑکا ہے	This is a boy.
4.	woh darwázá hā	وہ دروازہ ہے	That is a door.

27

5.	yēh ádmi hā	یہ آدمی ہے	This is a man.
6.	woh áurat hā	وہ عورت ہے	That is a woman.
7.	woh larki hā	وہ لڑکی ہے	That is a girl.
8.	yēh ghari hā	یہ گھڑی ہے	This is a watch.
9.	woh darakht hā	وہ درخت ہے	That is a tree.
10.	yēh kursi hā	یہ کرسی ہے	This is a chair.

VIII
Interrogative Sentences

In English, the interrogative sentences are formed by placing the auxiliary verb in the beginning of the sentences, but in Urdu, it is done by adding "kiā" (کیا) in the beginning of the sentences, as shown below:

	Urdu		*English*
1.	kiá yēh kitab hā?	کیا یہ کتاب ہے ؟	Is this a book?
2.	kiá woh mēz hā?	کیا وہ میز ہے ؟	Is that a table?
3.	kiá woh larká hā?	کیا وہ لڑکا ہے ؟	Is he a boy?
4.	kiá woh darwázá hā?	کیا وہ دروازہ ہے ؟	Is that a door?

EXERCISE 1

Inflections of the verb honá (ہونا) "to be"

	Urdu		*English*
1.	Māň ádmi hooň	میں آدمی ہوں۔	I am a man.
2.	Tum dhobi ho	تم دھوبی ہو۔	You are a washerman.
3.	Woh larká hā	وہ لڑکا ہے۔	He is a boy.
4.	Woh larki hā	وہ لڑکی ہے ۔	She is a girl.
5.	Woh máli hāň	وہ مالی ہے۔	He is a gardener.
6.	Too bachchá hā	تو بچہ ہے ۔	Thou art a child.
7.	Áp ustád hāň	آپ استاد میں۔	You are a teacher.
8.	Ham naukar hāň	ہم نوکر میں	We are servants.
9.	Kiá tum naukar ho?	کیا تم نوکر ہو ؟	Are you a servant?
10.	Māň naukar naheeň hun	میں نوکر نہیں ہوں	I am not a servant.

28

11. Kiá áp ustád hāǹ, کیا آپ استاد میں، Are you a teacher?

12. Gi háǹ, māǹ ustad hoon جی ہاں میں استاد ہوں Yes sir, I am a teacher.

EXERCISE 2

1. Yēh mērá qalam hā. یہ میرا قلم ہے۔
2. Woh meri kitáb hā. وہ میری کتاب ہے۔
3. Yēh hamárá daftar hā. یہ ہمارا دفتر ہے۔
4. Yēh hamári dukán hā. یہ ہماری دکان ہے۔
5. Kiá woh tumhárá makán hā? کیا وہ تمہارا مکان ہے؟
6. Naheeǹ, woh mera makán naheeǹ hā. نہیں، وہ میرا مکان نہیں ہے۔
7. Yēh uska akbár hā. یہ اس کا اخبار ہے۔
8. Kiá woh hamári library hā? کیا وہ ہماری لائبریری ہے؟
9. Háǹ, woh hamári library hā. ہاں وہ ہماری لائبریری ہے۔
10. Yēh tērá tálá hā. یہ تیرا تالا ہے۔

EXERCISE 3

1. Kitáb mēz par hā. کتاب میز پر ہے۔
2. Ádmi daryá meñ hā. آدمی دریا میں ہے۔
3. Páni gláss mēǹ hā. پانی گلاس میں ہے۔
4. Kursi ghar mēǹ hā. کرسی گھر میں ہے۔
5. School sē ghar tak. سکول سے گھر تک۔
6. Lahore sē Karachi ko. لاہور سے کراچی کو۔

EXERCISE 4: Mixed Sentences

1. Woh dák káná hā. وہ ڈاک خانہ ہے۔
2. Yēh chábi naheeǹ, tálá hā. یہ چابی نہیں، تالا ہے۔
3. Yēh mēz hā, kursi naheeǹ. یہ میز ہے، کرسی نہیں۔
4. Kiá kitáb farsh per hā? کیا کتاب فرش پر ہے؟
5. Ji naheeǹ, mēz per hā. جی نہیں، میز پر ہے۔
6. Kiá yēh charpáec naheeǹ hā? کیا یہ چارپائی نہیں ہے؟

29

7. Naheeň, yēh mēz hā. نہیں یہ میز ہے۔

8. Doodh thandá hā. دودھ ٹھنڈا ہے۔

9. Cháē garm hā. چائے گرم ہے۔

10. Kitáb sabz hā aur qalam surkh hā. کتاب سبز ہے اور قلم سرخ ہے۔

11. Darakt baṛá hā aur pauḍá chotá hā. درخت بڑا ہے اور پودا چھوٹا ہے۔

12. Larki khoobsoorat hā aur larká badsoorat hā. لڑکی خوبصورت ہے اور لڑکا بدصورت ہے۔

13. Mēri jēb mēñ kághz hā. میری جیب میں کاغذ ہے۔

14. Mērē hath mēñ phool hā. میرے ہاتھ میں پھول ہے۔

15. Uski qameez nei hā. اس کی قمیض نئی ہے۔

16. Uskā pen nayá hā. اس کا پن نیا ہے۔

17. Hamárá ghar college sē ḍoor hā. ہمارا گھر کالج سے دور ہے۔

18. Ápká nám kiá hā. آپ کا نام کیا ہے؟

19. Yēh kitáb achchi hā aur woh akbár gandá hā. یہ کتاب اچھی ہے اور وہ اخبار گندہ ہے۔

20. Cháqoo tēz hā aur churi kunḍ hā. چاقو تیز ہے اور چھری کند ہے۔

21. Māň tálib ilm hooň. میں طالب علم ہوں۔

22. Tum máli ho. تم مالی ہو۔

23. Áp ustád háň. آپ استاد ہیں۔

24. Too chotá larká hā. تو چھوٹا لڑکا ہے۔

25. Ham bágh mēň háň. ہم باغ میں ہیں۔

IX

Use of "Tha" (تھا) and "Thē" (تھے)

'Thá' is the past tense of "hā" and 'thē' is the past tense of "háň". Their use is illustrated by the following examples:

English	Urdu	
1. He was a servant.	Woh naukar thá.	وہ نوکر تھا۔
2. They were servants.	Woh naukar thē.	وہ نوکر تھے۔
3. I was a student.	Māň tálib ilm thá.	میں طالب علم تھا۔
4. You were students.	Tum tálib ilm thē.	تم طالب علم تھے۔

5. We were shopkeepers.   Ham ḍukándár thē.   ہم دوکاندار تھے۔

In English 'was' and 'were' are used both for males and females, but in Urdu 'thā' changes into 'thi' for female singulars and 'thi' becomes 'theñ' for female plurals. Its examples will be given at a later stage when the students have learnt the formation of genders and numbers.

X

Interrogative Words

The word used in a question is called the 'interrogative' word. The following words serve the purpose of asking questions in Urdu, the English equivalents of which are given against each word:

Urdu		English
1. Kiá	کیا	What
2. Kaun	کون	Who
3. Kāsē	کیسے	How
4. Kaháñ	کہاں	Where
5. Kioñ	کیوں	Why
6. Kab	کب	When

In Urdu, interrogative words always come just before the verb, as shown in the following examples:

1. Áp ká nám kiá hā?   آپ کا نام کیا ہے ؟
2. Ghar mēñ kaun hā?   گھر میں کون ہے ؟
3. Áp kāsē hāñ?   آپ کیسے ہیں ؟
4. Tum ájkal kaháñ ho?   تم آج کل کہاں ہو ؟
5. Laṛke khush kioñ hāñ?   لڑکے خوش کیوں ہیں ؟
6. Uská imtēhán kab hā?   اس کا امتحان کب ہے ؟

31

Chapter III
GENDERS AND NUMBERS

I
Gender

Masculine and Feminine

Unlike English, there are two genders in Urdu i.e., masculine and feminine; there being no neuter gender in it. There is no fixed rule for identifying the gender of non living (inanimate) objects, which is to be learnt by heart in every individual case.

The form of verb in Urdu, unlike English, corresponds to the gender of the noun it qualifies.

Generally nouns ending with a long á (ا) are masculines and those ending with 'ee' or 'i' (ی) are feminines, as shown by the following examples:

	Masculine		Feminine	
1.	Larká	لڑکا	Larki	لڑکی
2.	Kamrá	کمرہ	Lakri	لکڑی
3.	Darwázá	دروازہ	Khirki	کھڑکی
4.	Sheeshá	شیشہ	Topi	ٹوپی
5.	Kuttá	کتّا	Gali	گلی
6.	Kaprá	کپڑا	Kursi	کرسی
7.	Ghorá	گھوڑا	Ghori	گھوڑی
8.	Bakrá	بکرا	Bakri	بکری

But there are exceptions to this rule. For instance, ádmi (آدمی), páni (پانی), bháee (بھائی), háthi (ہاتھی), mali (مالی), etc. all end with ee or i (ی) but they are masculines.

32

II

Number

Singular and Plural

In Urdu, as in English, there are two kinds of numbers, singular and plural; the former denoting one and the latter more than one thing.

Singular nouns are changed into plural nouns according to the following rules.

Nouns Followed by Postpositions

1. If a noun, whether masculine or feminine, is followed by a postposition; its plural is made by adding "oñ" (وں) to it, as illustrated below:

	Singular		*Plural*
1.	Kitáb	کتاب	Kitáb + oñ = Kitáboñ
2.	Mez	میز	Mēz + oñ = Mēzoñ
3.	Kursi	کرسی	Kursi + oñ = Kursioñ
4.	Khat	خط	Khat + oñ = Khatoñ

2. If a noun ends with a long á (ا or ہ), it is changed into plural after dropping the long á (ا or ہ):

	Singular		*Plural*	
1.	Kamrá	کمرا	Kamr + oñ = Kamroñ	کمروں
2.	Larká	لڑکا	Lark + oñ = Larkoñ	لڑکوں
3.	Darwázá	دروازہ	Darwáz + oñ = Darwázoñ	دروازوں
4.	Sheeshá	شیشہ	Sheesh + oñ = Sheeshoñ	شیشوں

Nouns Not Followed by Postpositions

1.   If a masculine noun is not followed by a postposition and does not end with a long á (‌ا or ه), it is used both as singular and plural, the number of the verb indicating the number of the noun it qualifies, as   illustrated below:

	Singular			Plural	
1.	Woh ádmi hā.	وہ آدمی ہے		Woh ádmi hāṅ.	وہ آدمی ہیں ۔
2.	Yēh pen hā.	یہ پن ہے		Yēh pen hāṅ.	یہ پن ہیں ۔
3.	Yēh hath hā.	یہ ہاتھ ہے		Yēh hath hāṅ.	یہ ہاتھ ہیں ۔

2.   If a masculine noun ends with a long 'á' (‌ہا or ه), it is replaced by 'ē' (ے), as illustrated below:

	Singular			Plural	
1.	Ghorá	گھوڑا		Ghorē	گھوڑے
2.	Kuttá	کتّا		Kuttē	کتّے
3.	Kamrá	کمرہ		Kamrē	کمرے
4.	Darwázá	دروازہ		Darwázē	دروازے

3.   If a feminine noun ends with 'i' or 'ee' (ی), its plural is made by adding 'áṅ' to it, as illustrated below:

	Singular		Plural	
1.	Larki	لڑکی	Larki + áṅ = Larkiáṅ	لڑکیاں
2.	Beevi	بیوی	Beevi + áṅ = Beeviáṅ	بیویاں
3.	Kursi	کرسی	Kursi + áṅ = Kursiáṅ	کرسیاں
4.	Ghori	گھوڑی	Ghori + áṅ = Ghoriáṅ	گھوڑیاں

4.   If a feminine noun ends with a long 'á' (‌ا), its plural is made by adding nasal 'ṅ' (ں) to it, as under:

34

	Singular		Plural	
1.	Guṛiá	گُڑیا	+ ň = Guṛiáň	گُڑیاں
2.	Chiṛiá	چِڑیا	+ ň = Chiṛiáň	چِڑیاں
3.	Puṛiá	پُڑیا	+ ň = Puṛiáň	پُڑیاں

5. If a feminine noun ends with any letter except 'i' (ی)
or long á (ا), its plural is made by adding "ēň" (یں) to it, as is
shown by the following examples:

	Singular		Plural	
1.	Behen	بہن	+ ēň = Behenēň	بہنیں
2.	Qameez	قمیض	+ ēň = Qameezēň	قمیضیں
3.	Áňkh	آنکھ	+ ēň = Áňkhēň	آنکھیں
4.	Botal	بوتل	+ ēň = Botalēň	بوتلیں
5.	Mez	میز	+ ēň = Mezēň	میزیں

III
Genetive Case

A genetive case denotes the class or kind to which a thing
belongs. It is expressed by the word "of" or the mark of comma "
over 's' called apostrophe ('S). In Urdu, ká (کا), ki (کی) or kē
(کے) are used for denoting the genetive case, as illustrated by the
following examples:

	English	Urdu	
1.	Owner of the book	Kitáb ká málik (Book's owner)	کتاب کا مالک
2.	Door of the house	Ghar ká darwázá (House's door)	گھر کا دروازہ
3.	Box of the servant	Naukar ká sandooq (Servant's box)	نوکر کا صندوق
4.	House of the friend	Dost ká makán (Friend's house)	دوست کا مکان
5.	Room of the Hotel	Hotel ká kamrá (Hotel's room)	ہوٹل کا کمرہ

If the noun following 'ká' is feminine or plural, 'ká' changes
into 'ki' and 'kē' respectively, as shown by the following examples:

35

English	Urdu	
1. Owners of the shop	Dukán kē málik	دُکان کے مالک
2. Doors of the house	Makán kē darwázē	مکان کے دروازے۔
3. Key of the lock	Tálē ki chábi	تالے کی چابی
4. Watch of the woman	Áurat ki ghaṛi	عورت کی گھڑی

EXERCISE I

1. Woh larkē hāṅ. — وہ لڑکے ہیں
2. Woh larkiáṅ hāṅ. — وہ لڑکیاں ہیں
3. Áuratēṅ kaháṅ hāṅ? — عورتیں کہاں ہیں ؟
4. Kitábēṅ mēzoṅ par hāṅ. — کتابیں میزوں پر ہیں۔
5. Kursiáṅ kamroṅ mēṅ hāṅ. — کرسیاں کمروں میں ہیں۔
6. Áuratēṅ gharoṅ mēṅ hāṅ. — عورتیں گھروں میں ہیں۔
7. Kamroṅ mēṅ kaun hāṅ? — کمروں میں کون ہیں ؟
8. Larkē school mēṅ hāṅ. — لڑکے سکول میں ہیں۔
9. Gáriaṅ saṛakoṅ par hāṅ. — گاڑیاں سڑکوں پر ہیں
10. Kaprē dukánoṅ mēṅ hāṅ. — کپڑے دُکانوں میں ہیں۔

EXERCISE II

1. Áp ká nám kiá hā? — آپ کا نام کیا ہے ؟
2. Ghar ká málik kaun hā? — گھر کا مالک کون ہے ؟
3. Dukán kē darwázē khoobsoorat hāṅ. — دکان کے دروازے خوبصورت ہیں
4. Yēh áurat ki kitáb hā. — یہ عورت کی کتاب ہے۔
5. Yēh ádmi ki qameez hā. — یہ آدمی کی قمیض ہے۔
6. Larki kē bál kalē hāṅ. — لڑکی کے بال کالے ہیں۔
7. Bulb ki raushni kam hā. — بلب کی روشنی کم ہے۔
8. Masjid kē minár safád hāṅ. — مسجد کے مینار سفید ہیں۔
9. Khirki ká sheesha sáf naheeṅ. — کھڑکی کا شیشہ صاف نہیں۔
10. Mēzon kē kaprē gandē hāṅ. — میزوں کے کپڑے گندے ہیں۔

36

Chapter IV

TENSES

Infinitives

In Urdu, as we have seen in Chapter II, all infinitives end with 'ná' (‬), as they precede by "to" in English. The following examples illustrate this point:

	Urdu		English
1.	áná	آنا	to come
2.	jáná	جانا	to go
3.	kháná	کھانا	to eat
4.	soná	سونا	to sleep
5.	likhná	لکھنا	to write
6.	parhná	پڑھنا	to read
7.	bathná	بیٹھنا	to sit
8.	chalná	چلنا	to walk
9.	dorná	دوڑنا	to run
10.	peená	پینا	to drink

Imperatives

An imperative mood is the form of a verb expressing command, advice or request.

In Urdu, an imperative is formed by dropping 'ná' (‬) occurring at the end of an infinitive as shown by the following examples:

Infintive		Imperative	
Áná	آنا	Á	آ
Jáná	جانا	Ja	جا
Kháná	کھانا	Khá	کھا
Soná	سونا	So	سو

The á, já, khá and so are crude forms of imperatives and are generally used for servants and menials. It is rude to address others like this, except frank friends.

II

Polite Forms

From the crude imperatives, polite forms are formed as under:

Infinitive	Imperative		
	Crude	Polite	Very Polite
1. Likhná لکھنا	Likh لکھ	Likho لکھو	Likhiyē کھیے
2. Parhná پڑھنا	Parh پڑھ	Parho پڑھو	Parhiyē پڑھیے
3. Áná آنا	Á آ	Áo آؤ	Áiyē آیئے
4. Jáná جانا	Já جا	Jáo جاؤ	Jáiyē جایئے
5. Uthná اٹھنا	Uth اٹھ	Utho اٹھو	Uthiyē اٹھیے
6. Bhējná بھیجنا	Bhej بھیج	Bhejo بھیجو	Bhejiyē بھیجیے
7. Bolná بولنا	Bol بول	Bolo بولو	Boliyē بولیے
8. Milná ملنا	Mil مل	Milo ملو	Miliyē ملیے
9. Dekhná دیکھنا	Dekh دیکھ	Dekho دیکھو	Dekhiyē دیکھیے
10. Daurná دوڑنا	Daur دوڑ	Dauro دوڑو	Dauriyē دوڑیے
11. Girná گرنا	Gir گر	Giro گرو	Giriyē گریے
12. Kehná کہنا	Keh کہ	Kaho کہو	Kahiyē کہیے
13. Khareedná خریدنا	Khareed خرید	Khareedo خریدو	Khareediyē خریدیے

The second form of imperative is generally used for equals but the third form is used for people of all age groups, without any restrictions, whether they may be superiors or inferiors.

Notes: (1) From the infinitives ḍená, lená, karná and peená, the third (very polite) form of the imperatives is slightly irregular. It is deejiyē (دیجیے), leejiyē (لیجیے), keejiyē (کیجیے) and peejiyē (پیجیے), respectively.

(2) The pronouns too (تو), tum (تم) and áp (آپ) should be used with the first, second and third forms of the imperatives, respectively. However, the pronoun may be omitted, if desired.

EXERCISE

1. Tum school ko jāo. تم سکول کو جاؤ
2. Áp kitáb paṛhiyē. آپ کتاب پڑھیے
3. Tu kapi par likh. تو کاپی پر لکھ
4. Ghar mēň áiyē. گھر میں آئیے
5. Naukar ko dukán par bhējiyē. نوکر کو دکان پر بھیجیے ۔
6. Kitáb mēz par rakhiyē. کتاب میز پر رکھیے
7. Kursi par bethiyē. کرسی پر بیٹھیے
8. Jaldi jáo aur bázár sē kaghẓ láo. جلدی جاؤ اور بازار سے کاغذ لاؤ
9. Qalam jēb mēň ḍálo. قلم جیب میں ڈالو
10. Cháē mēň cheeni ḍálo aur chamach sē hiláo. چائے میں چینی ڈالو اور چمچ سے ہلاؤ
11. Bazár sē phal láo. بازار سے پھل لاؤ
12. Thandá páni peejiyē. ٹھنڈا پانی پیجیے
13. Garm roti kháiyē. گرم روٹی کھائیے
14. Kitab leejiyē aur dost ko ḍeejiyē. کتاب لیجیے اور دوست کو دیجیے ۔
15. Áhista chaliyē. آہستہ چلیے

39

III
Past Tense
Past Indefinite

The first form of imperative (crude form) is made by dropping 'ná' (نا), occurring at the end of an infinitive. For example, from soná, áná and bethná we get so, á and beth as imperatives, respectively.

Add long 'á' (ا) to this crude form and we get the past indefinite tense, as is illustrated by the following examples:

	Infinitive		Crude Imperative		Past Indefinite	
1.	Bāthná	بیٹھنا	Bāth	بیٹھ	Bāthá	بیٹھا
2.	Daurná	دوڑنا	Dauṛ	دوڑ	Dauṛá	دوڑا
3.	Likhná	لکھنا	Likh	لکھ	Likhá	لکھا
4.	Parhná	پڑھنا	Paṛh	پڑھ	Paṛhá	پڑھا
5.	Jágná	جاگنا	Jág	جاگ	Jágá	جاگا

But, if the crude imperative ends with a vowel, add yá (یا) to it: examples:

	Infinitive		Crude Imperative		Past Indefinite	
1.	Áná	آنا	Á	آ	Áyá	آیا
2.	Kháná	کھانا	Khá	کھا	Kháyá	کھایا
3.	Soná	سونا	So	سو	Soyá	سویا
4.	Roná	رونا	Ro	رو	Royá	رویا
5.	Peena	پینا	Pee	پی	Peeyá	پیا

In some cases past indefinite tense is made in an irregular way, for example, the past indefinite of 'karná' (کرنا) is 'kiyá' (کیا) and 'janá' (جانا) is 'gayá' (گیا).

IV
Transitives and Intransitives
Intransitive Verb

In the past tense, verbs are of two kinds, transitive and intransitive. The action of the intransitive verb terminates at the

subject. In other words, the sentence appears to be complete
without object.

Examples

	Urdu		English
1.	Woh ḍauṛá	وہ دوڑا	He ran.
2.	Larká soyá	لڑکا سویا	The boy slept.
3.	Ahmed gayá	احمد گیا	Ahmed went.

The number and gender of the intransitive verb invariably
agrees with the number and gender of the subject used in a
sentence, as shown by the following examples:

Infinitive	Impera-tive	Singular		Plural	
		Male	Female	Male	Female
1. Ánā آنا	Á آ	Ayá آیا	Aee آئی	Aē آۓ	Áeeň آئیں
2. Roná رونا	Ro رو	Rová رویا	Roee روئی	Roē روۓ	Roeeň روئیں
3. Bāthná بیٹھنا	Bāth بیٹھ	Bāthá بیٹھا	Bāthi بیٹھی	Bāthē بیٹھے	Bātheeň بیٹھیں
4. Jáná جانا	Já جا	Gayá گیا	Gāee گئی	Gaē گۓ	Gaeeň گئیں

EXERCISE

1. Hamári gáṛi kahan gaee?   ہماری گاڑی کہاں گئی ،
2. Maň kal Lahore gayá.   میں کل لاہور گیا۔
3. Tum ḍaftar sē kab ayē?   تم دفتر سے کب آۓ ؟
4. Naukar ḍarzi sē kapṛē layá.   نوکر درزی سے کپڑے لایا
5. Larkē bágh mēň gayē.   لڑکے باغ میں آۓ۔

6. Larkián school sē áeeň.   لڑکیاں سکول سے آئیں۔

7. Áurateň bázár sē kaprá láeen.   عورتیں بازار سے کپڑا لائیں۔

8. Áp waháň dost sē milē.   آپ وہاں دوست سے ملے

9. Ham station par der sē pohnchē.   ہم سٹیشن پر دیر سے پہنچے۔

10. Maň áj rát ko der sē soyá.   میں آج رات کو دیر سے سویا۔

V

Transitive Verb

The meaning of a transitive verb is complete only when its object is mentioned in the sentence. In such sentences the gender and number of the object determines the gender and number of the verb.

In transitive past tense subject is followed by 'nē' (نے) which means 'by'. 'Woh' (وہ) changes into 'us' (اُس) and 'yēh' (یہ) becomes 'is' (اِس), with 'unhoň' (انہوں) as their plural.

The following examples illustrate these points:

	English	*Urdu*	
1.	He said. (Said by him.)	Us nē kahá.	اُس نے کہا
2.	They said. (Said by them.)	Unhoň nē kahá.	انہوں نے کہا
3.	You said. (Said by you.)	Tum nē kahá.	تم نے کہا
	You said. (Said by you.) (honorific)	Áp nē kahá.	آپ نے کہا
4.	I said. (Said by me.)	Meň nē kahá.	میں نے کہا
5.	We said. (Said by us.)	Ham nē kahá.	ہم نے کہا

Examples in Sentences

1. Ustád nē qalam khareedá.   استاد نے قلم خریدا
2. Ustád nē kitáb parhi.   استاد نے کتاب پڑھی
3. Larki nē ghori dekhi.   لڑکی نے گھوڑی دیکھی
4. Larki nē ghorá dekhá.   لڑکی نے گھوڑا دیکھا

5. Áuraṭ nē kiṭab paṛhi.   عورت نے کتاب پڑھی

6. Áuraṭ nē kiṭabēṅ parheeṅ.   عورت نے کتابیں پڑھیں

7. Larkoṅ nē sabaq paṛhá.   لڑکوں نے سبق پڑھا

8. Docṭor nē dawá di.   ڈاکٹر نے دوا دی

9. Docṭor nē dawáēṅ deeṅ.   ڈاکٹر نے دوائیں دیں ۔

10. Kuṭṭē nē goshṭ khayá.   کتے نے گوشت کھایا

11. Kuṭṭoṅ nē goshṭ khayá.   کتوں نے گوشت کھایا

12. Tum nē akhbár paṛhá.   تم نے اخبار پڑھا ۔

EXERCISE

Past Indefinite of Transitive Verb

1. Meṅ nē risálá paṛhá.   میں نے رسالہ پڑھا ۔

2. Ham nē kiṭabēṅ parheeṅ.   ہم نے کتابیں پڑھیں ۔

3. Nauker nē chaē pi.   نوکر نے چائے پی

4. Ádmi nē ghorē dekhē.   آدمی نے گھوڑے دیکھے

5. Áurtoṅ nē ghorē dekhē.   عورتوں نے گھوڑے دیکھے ۔

6. Mēṅ nē darakhṭ katá.   میں نے درخت کاٹا

7. Mēṅ nē darakhṭ katē.   میں نے درخت کاٹے

8. Baṛá darwázá kis nē kholá?   بڑا دروازہ کس نے کھولا ؟

9. Chor nē ghari meri jēb sē nikáli.   چور نے گھڑی میری جیب سے نکالی ۔

10. Tum nē sáṅp dekha.   تم نے سانپ دیکھا

11. Tum nē do sáṅp dēkhe.   تم نے دو سانپ دیکھے

12. Ham nē bazár sē kia khareedá?   ہم نے بازار سے کیا خریدا ؟

13. Ham nē topi khareedi.   ہم نے ٹوپی خریدی

14. Mēṅ nē kághz par likhá aur tum nē parhá.   میں نے کاغذ پر لکھا اور تم نے پڑھا

15. Ustád nē bachchoṅ ko kahániaṅ sunáeeṅ.   استاد نے بچوں کو کہانیاں سنائیں

16. Máṅ nē bachchē ko kahání sunáee.   ماں نے بچے کو کہانی سنائی ۔

17. Bap nē betē ko ek roopiá diá.   باپ نے بیٹے کو ایک روپیہ دیا

18. Larki nē cháē naheeṅ pee.   لڑکی نے چائے نہیں پی ۔

19. Larki nē páni naheeṅ piá.   لڑکی نے پانی نہیں پیا

20. Ádmi nē roti naheeṅ kháee.   آدمی نے روٹی نہیں کھائی ۔

VI
Past Perfect Tense

When somebody says, "I saw him," it is clear that the action took place in the past, but when exactly did it take place, is not clear from it, and so it is called past indefinite (imperfect) tense; but when someone says, "I have seen him," it means that the action took place in the near past. Likewise, when somebody says, "I had seen him," it means that he saw him in the distant past.

In Urdu, unlike English, past indefinite is not much in use; hence past perfect, both of near and distant type, assumes greater importance as it is more common in speech and writing.

It is made as under:

Add 'hā' (ﮯ) or 'haṅ' (ﮟ) according to the number desired, to the past indefinite tense of a transitive or intransitive verb for making the past perfect tense of the near type.

Add 'thá' (ﺗﮭﺎ) or 'thē' (ﺗﮭﮯ) to the past indefinite tense according to the number desired, if the verb denotes masculine gender; for making a past perfect tense of the distant type.

If the verb denotes faminine gender, add 'thee' (ﺗﮭﻰ) or 'theeṅ' (ﺗﮭﯿﮟ) according to the number desired.

When 'háṅ' (ﮟ) or 'theeṅ' (ﺗﮭﯿﮟ) is added to the verb in feminine gender, the plural form of the past indefinite tense is changed into singular.

The following examples illustrate the use of past perfect tense of near type, made from the transitive verbs:

	Past Indefinite Tense	*Past Perfect Tense*
1.	Mēṅ nē kitáb parhi. میں نے کتاب پڑھی	Meṅ nē kitáb parhi hā. میں نے کتاب پڑھی ہے
2.	Nauker nē darakht kátá. نوکر نے درخت کاٹا	Nauker nē darakht kátá hā. نوکر نے درخت کاٹا ہے
3.	Darwázá kis nē kholá? دروازہ کس نے کھولا؟	Darwázá kis nē kholá hā? دروازہ کس نے کھولا ہے ؟

44

4. Tum nē khat kioň likhá?	Tum nē khat kioň likha hā?
تم نے خط کیوں لکھا ؟	تم نے خط کیوں لکھا ہے ؟
5. Ustád nē topi pehni.	Ustad nē topi pehni hā.
استاد نے ٹوپی پہنی	استاد نے ٹوپی پہنی ہے
6. Dhobi nē kaprē dhoē.	Dhobi nē kaprē dhoē háň.
دھوبی نے کپڑے دھوئے	دھوبی نے کپڑے دھوئے ہیں ۔

Examples of the Past Perfect (Distant Type)

Past Indefinite Tense	*Past Perfect (Distant)*
1. Mēň nē kitáb parhi.	Mēň nē kitáb parhi thi.
میں نے کتاب پڑھی	میں نے کتاب پڑھی تھی
2. Mēň nē kitábēň parheeň.	Mēň nē kitábēň parhi theeň.
میں نے کتابیں پڑھیں	میں نے کتابیں پڑھی تھیں
3. Ham nē gáná gáyá.	Ham nē gáná gáyá thá.
ہم نے گانا گایا	ہم نے گانا گایا تھا
4. Dukándár nē topiaň bēcheeň.	Dukándár nē topiaň bēchi theeň.
دکاندار نے ٹوپیاں بیچیں	دکاندار نے ٹوپیاں بیچی تھیں
5. Billi nē doodh piyá.	Billi nē doodh piyá thá.
بلی نے دودھ پیا	بلّی نے دودھ پیا تھا ۔
6. Dhobi nē kaprē dhoē.	Dhobi nē kaprē dhoē thē.
دھوبی نے کپڑے دھوئے	دھوبی نے کپڑے دھوئے تھے

EXERCISE

Past Perfect (Near and Distant Past)

1. Dukándár Karáchi gayá hā.
دکاندار کراچی گیا ہے ۔
2. Merá dost pichlē sál Karáchi gayá thá.
میرا دوست پچھلے سال کراچی گیا تھا۔
3. Mãň kal school naheeň gayá thá.
میں کل سکول نہیں گیا تھا ۔
4. Larki áj college gei hā.
لڑکی آج کالج گئی ہے ۔

45

5. Larká áj college naheeň gayá.[1] رُڑکا آج کالج نہیں گیا۔

6. Áp England kab gaē thē? آپ انگلینڈ کب گۓ تھے ؟

7. Merá bháee America sē ayá hā. میرا بھائی امریکہ سے آیا ہے۔

8. Naukar kamrē mēň ayá thá
   aur mēň bahar gayá thá. نوکر کمرے میں آیا تھا اور میں باہر گیا تھا ۔

9. Police nē áj ēk chor pakrá hā. پولیس نے آج ایک چور پکڑا ہے

10. Ustáni nē áj sabaq naheeň parhayá. استانی نے آج سبق نہیں پڑھایا

VII

Compound Verbs

Compound verbs are formed by prefixing the crude imperative of a verb to certain auxiliary (helping) verbs. With the crude imperatives of intransitive verbs, the past imperfect forms of jáná is generally used; whereas with the transitive verbs, the past imperfect forms of 'lená' or 'dená' are more commonly in use.

Examples

1. Bachchá thak gayá. (thak + gayá) بچہ تھک گیا۔

2. Dost á gayá. (á + gayá) دوست آگیا ۔

3. Naukar nē kám kar liyá. (kar + liyá) نوکر نے کام کرلیا۔

4. Kiá áp nē sabaq parh liyá. (parh + liyá) کیا آپ نے سبق پڑھ لیا ؟

5. Kiá us nē mērá kám kar diyá. (kar + diyá) کیا اُس نے میرا کام کردیا ؟

Past perfect tense, both of near and distant type, can also be made from compound verbs, as illustrated below:

---

1. In case of a negative sentence, the use of hā, hooň, ho, thá, thē, thi, etc. is not required at the end of the sentence.

46

EXERCISE:

1. Hamári gári kaun lēgayá hā?   ہماری گاڑی کون لے گیا ہے ؟
2. Mēň ab Karachi sē ágayá hooň.   میں اب کراچی سے آگیا ہوں ۔
3. Larki nē kitáb khareed li hā.   لڑکی نے کتاب خرید لی ہے ۔
4. Áurat nē risálá parh liyá hā.   عورت نے رسالہ پڑھ لیا ہے ۔
5. Kiá áp nē kaprē pehn liyē hāň.   کیا آپ نے کپڑے پہن لیے ہیں ؟
6. Dhobi nē kaprē dho liyē hāň.   دھوبی نے کپڑے دھو لیے ہیں ۔
7. Naukar nē meri qameez dhobi ko dē di hā.   نوکر نے میری قمیض دھوبی کو دے دی ہے ۔
8. Beevi nē bartan almari mēň rakh diyē hāň.   بیوی نے برتن الماری میں رکھ دیے ہیں ۔
9. Ham nē darwázá khol dia thá.   ہم نے دروازہ کھول دیا تھا ۔
10. Us nē kháná khá lia thá aur báhár chalá gayá thá.   اس نے کھانا کھا لیا تھا اور باہر چلا گیا تھا ۔

In place of gayá, liyá or diyá, sometimes 'chuká' is also used, which indicates that a certain action has completely finished.

Examples

1. Māň kot pehn chuká hooň.   میں کوٹ پہن چکا ہوں ۔
2. Larki kháná khá chuki hā.   لڑکی کھانا کھا چکی ہے ۔
3. Ham páni pi chukē hāň.   ہم پانی پی چکے ہیں ۔
4. Tum taqreer kar chukē ho.   تم تقریر کر چکے ہو ۔
5. Áurteň shehr chor chuki hāň.   عورتیں شہر چھوڑ چکی ہیں ۔

VIII
Present Indefinite Tense

We have seen in the preceding pages that the crude from of imperative is formed by dropping 'ná' (نا) occurring at the end of an infinitive. Add 'tá' (تا) for male singular; 'ti' (تی) for female singular and plural; and 'tē' (تے) for male plural; followed by the suffix "hā" (ہے), "hāň" (ہیں), "ho" (ہو) and "hooň" (ہوں), acording to the number and gender of the subject and you get the present indefinite tense

47

Its conjugation is as under:

	English	Urdu	
1.	The boy runs.	Laṛká doṛtá hā.	لڑکا دوڑتا ہے۔
2.	The girl runs.	Laṛki doṛti hā.	لڑکی دوڑتی ہے ۔
3.	You run. (masculine)	Tum doṛtē ho.	تم دوڑتے ہو۔
4.	You run. (feminine)	Tum doṛti ho.	تم دوڑتی ہو۔
5.	I run. (mas.)	Mēň doṛtá hooň.	میں دوڑتا ہوں
6.	I run. (fem.)	Mēň doṛti hooň.	میں دوڑتی ہوں
7.	We run. (mas.)	Ham doṛtē hāň.	ہم دوڑتے ہیں ۔
8.	We run. (fem.)	Ham doṛti hāň.	ہم دوڑتی ہیں ۔
9.	You run. (honorific/mas.)	Áp dortē hāň.	آپ دوڑتے ہیں ۔
10.	You run. (honorific/fem.)	Áp doṛti hāň.	آپ دوڑتی ہیں ۔

EXERCISE

1. Kuttá tez doṛtá hā.   کتّا تیز دوڑتا ہے ۔

2. Áurtēň khāná khāti hāň.   عورتیں کھانا کھاتی ہیں ۔

3. Dakiyá yahan kis waqt átá hā?   ڈاکیہ یہاں کس وقت آتا ہے ؟

4. Tum daftar sē kab átē ho?   تم دفتر سے کب آتے ہو؟

5. Ápki beti college sē kab áti hā?   آپکی بیٹی کالج سے کب آتی ہے ؟

6. Larkē kitáboň sē parhtē aur kápioň par likhtē hāň.   لڑکے کتابوں سے پڑھتے اور کاپیوں پر لکھتے ہیں ۔

7. Kiá áp ájkal cricket khēltē hāň?   کیا آپ آج کل کرکٹ کھیلتے ہیں ؟

8. Larki badminton naheeň khēlti.[1]   لڑکی بیڈمنٹن نہیں کھیلتی۔

9. Mēň ájkal football naheeň khēltá.   میں آج کل فٹ بال نہیں کھیلتا

10. Merá dost cigarette peetá hā aur mēň cháe peetá hooň   میرا دوست سیگرٹ پیتا ہے اور میں چائے پیتا ہوں

11. Áurat cháwal khāti hā aur ádmi roti khátá hā.   عورت چاول کھاتی ہے اور آدمی روٹی کھاتا ہے

12. Tum meri bát kioň nahceň samajtē?   تم میری بات کیوں نہیں سمجھتے ؟

13. Kiá áp károbár kartē hāň?   کیا آپ کاروبار کرتے ہیں ؟

---

1. In case of a negative sentence, hā, hāň, etc. can be dropped.

14. Woh abhi school meň paṛhti hā. دہ اسبھی سکول میں پڑھتی ہے ـ

15. Máli bághoň meň kám karte hāň aur مالی باغوں میں کام کرتے ہیں اور
unki áurteň gharoň meň kám karti hāň. انکی عورتیں گھروں میں کام کرتی ہیں ـ

IX
Present Continuous Tense

Present indefinite tense ends with "tá hā" (تا ہے), "ti hā"
(تی ہے), "tē hāň" (تے ہیں), and "ti hāň" (تی ہیں), according to the
gender and number of the subject. In the present continuous tense,
tá, ti and tē (تے ـ تی ـ تا) change into rahá, rahi and rahē
(رہا ـ رہی ـ رہے), respectively, as illustrated below:

	Present Indefinite	Present Continuous
1.	Māň játá hooň.	Māň já rahá hooň.
	میں جاتا ہوں	میں جا رہا ہوں
2.	Ham khaṭ likhtē hāň.	Ham khaṭ likh rahē hāň.
	ہم خط لکھتے ہیں	ہم خط لکھ رہے ہیں
3.	Áurteň kháná pakáti hāň.	Áurteň kháná paká rahi hāň.
	عورتیں کھانا پکاتی ہیں ـ	عورتیں کھانا پکا رہی ہیں
4.	Tum Urdu boltē ho.	Tum Urdu bol rahē ho.
	تم اردو بولتے ہو	تم اردو بول رہے ہو
5.	Áp kahaň jatē hāň?	Áp kahaň já rahē hāň?
	آپ کہاں جاتے ہیں	آپ کہاں جا رہے ہیں؟
6.	Bachchá toffee khátá hā.	Bachchá toffee khá rahá hā.
	بچہ ٹوفی کھاتا ہے	بچہ ٹوفی کھا رہا ہے ـ

EXERCISE

1. Woh bohat mehnat kar rahá hā. وہ بہت محنت کر رہا ہے ـ
2. Áurat doodh ubál rahi hā. عورت دودھ ابال رہی ہے ـ
3. Tum sabun sē háth dho rahē ho. تم صابن سے ہاتھ دھو رہے ہو ـ
4. Ham mádán meň cricket khel rahē hāň. ہم میدان میں کرکٹ کھیل رہے ہیں
5. Larkian dilchasp kahani sun rahi hāň. لڑکیاں دلچسپ کہانی سن رہی ہیں ـ
6. Áp mujh sē kuch chupá rahē hāň. آپ مجھ سے کچھ چھپا رہے ہیں ـ

49

7. Kiá woh abhi tak so rahē hāṅ? کیا وہ ابھی تک سو رہے ہیں ؟
8. Woh so naheeṅ rahē, jág rahē hāṅ. وہ سو نہیں رہے ، جاگ رہے ہیں ۔
9. Áp kiá kēh rahi hāṅ? آپ کیا کہہ رہی ہیں ؟
10. Māṅ kuch naheeṅ kēh rahi. میں کچھ نہیں کہہ رہی ۔

X
Past Imperfect

Present indefinite or imperfect tense ends with tá hā (تا ہے), ti hā (تی ہے), tē hāṅ (تے ہیں) and ti hāṅ (تی ہیں) according to the gender and number of the subject. Replace 'hā' (ہے) and its other inflections by thá (تھا) and its various inflections and you get past imperfect tense, as under:

	Present Imperfect	*Past Imperfect*
1.	Woh Lahore játá hā. وہ لاہور جاتا ہے	Woh Lahore játá thá. وہ لاہور جاتا تھا
2.	Tum gáná gátē ho. تم گانا گاتے ہو ۔	Tum gáná gátē thē. تم گانا گاتے تھے
3.	Larkē kitábēṅ parhtē hāṅ. لڑکے کتابیں پڑھتے ہیں	Larkē kitábēṅ parhtē thē. لڑکے کتابیں پڑھتے تھے
4.	Larkiáṅ kitábēṅ parhti hāṅ. لڑکیاں کتابیں پڑھتی ہیں	Larkiáṅ kitábēṅ parhti theeṅ. لڑکیاں کتابیں پڑھتی تھیں
5.	Larkiáṅ soti hāṅ. لڑکیاں سوتی ہیں ۔	Larkiáṅ soti theeṅ. لڑکیاں سوتی تھیں

XI
Past Imperfect (Continuous)

Present imperfect continuous tense changes into past imperfect continuous, if hā (ہے) and its other inflections are replaced by "thá" (تھا) and its other inflections, as under:

	Present Imperfect (Continuous)	*Past Imperfect (Continuous)*
1.	Woh Lahore já rahá hā.	Woh Lahore já rahá thá.

2. Tum gáná gá rahē ho.   Tum gáná gá rahē thē.

تم گانا گا رہے تے   تم گانا گا رہے تے

3. Laṛki kitáb paṛh rahi hā.   Laṛki kitáb paṛh rahi thi.

لڑکی کتاب پڑھ رہی ہے   لڑکی کتاب پڑھ رہی تھی

4. Laṛkiáṅ so rahi hāṅ.   Laṛkiáṅ so rahi theeṅ.

لڑکیاں سو رہی ہیں   لڑکیاں سو رہی تھیں

XII

Perpetual Present and Past

Perpetual present and past tenses are not much in use in English. In Urdu, also it has lost much of its pristine force. However, rarely, it is still in use.

Present perpetual tense is made by adding past participle to the present indefinite tense, which in English means, "I am in habit of doing."

For past perpetual tense we should replace 'hā' (ہے) and its other inflections by 'thá' (تھا) and its various inflections. Habitual past tense, in English, is sometimes expressed as: "I used to do."

Examples

Perpetual Present Tense	*Perpetual Past Tense*
1. Larká jáyá kartá hā.	Larká jáyá kartá thá.
لڑکا جایا کرتا ہے	لڑکا جایا کرتا تھا
2. Woh dopehr ko soyá kartá hā.	Woh dopehr ko soyá kartá thá.
وہ دوپہر کو سویا کرتا ہے	وہ دوپہر کو سویا کرتا تھا
3. Tum gáná gáyá kartē ho.	Tum gáná gáyá kartē thē.
تم گانا گایا کرتے ہو	تم گانا گایا کرتے تے
4. Laṛkiáṅ khelá karti hāṅ.	Laṛkiáṅ khelá karti theeṅ.
لڑکیاں کھیلا کرتی ہیں	لڑکیاں کھیلا کرتی تھیں

51

5. Mãň har roz sar kiá kartá
   hooň.

   میں ہر روز سیر کیا کرتا ہوں

   Mãň har roz sar kiá kartá thá.

   میں ہر روز سیر کیا کرتا تھا

6. Ham shám ko cháē piá
   kartē hāň.

   ہم شام کو چائے پیا کرتے ہیں

   Ham shám ko cháē pigá
   kartē thē.

   ہم شام کو چائے پیا کرتے تھے

7. Áp rát ko cháwal khayá
   kartē hāň.

   آپ رات کو چاول کھایا کرتے ہیں

   Áp rát ko cháwal khayá
   kartē thē.

   آپ رات کو چاول کھایا کرتے تھے

Perpetual present tense sometimes, assumes the following
form:

1. Mãň sār kartá rehtá hooň.   میں سیر کرتا رہتا ہوں

2. Ham shám ko cháē peetē rehtē hāň.   ہم شام کو چائے پیتے رہتے ہیں

This form of present perpetual tense can be changed into
perpetual past tense by the usual method, described above.

XIII
Aorist Tense

In Urdu, unlike English, aorist tense is much in use. In
English, it has only one shade of meaning, that is of the weak and
mild "can": he may go, they may write, you may sit, etc. In Urdu, it
has many shades of meaning. It is also helpful in making some
forward forms of tenses.

How is it made?

Add 'ē' (ے), 'eň' (یں), 'o' (و) and 'ooň' (وں)
according to the number of the subject, to the crude imperative of a
verb and you get the aorist tense. It is the same for any of the two
genders, as explained below:

Subject	Imperative	Aorist
Larká/Larki	á (from áná)	á + ē = áē آ ئے

Larkē/Larkiañ	já (from jáná)	já + ēñ = jáēñ جائیں
Tum (mas. and fem.)	khá (from kháná)	khá + o = kháo کھاؤ
Māñ (mas. and fem.)	chal (from chalná)	chal + ooñ = chalooñ چلوں
Ham (mas. and fem.)	daur (from daurná)	daur + ēñ = daurēñ دوڑیں
Áp (mas. and fem.)	so (from soná)	so + ēñ = soēñ سوئیں

The various shades of meaning of the aorist tense in Urdu have been illustrated below:

Urdu	*English*
1. Áo! ham náshtá karēñ. آؤ ہم ناشتہ کریں	Come! let us take breakfast.
2. Utho! abhi bázár chalēñ. اُٹھو! ابھی بازار چلیں	Get up! let us go to bazar right now.
3. Ham thak gaē hāñ, ab árám karēñ. ہم تھک گئے ہیں، اب آرام کریں	We are tired, let us take rest now.

Aorist is used in the sense of 'may' and 'might' also. The word sháyad (شاید), meaning perhaps, is used in the beginning of such sentences:

Urdu	*English*
1. Sháyad māñ áj usko kat likhooñ. شاید میں آج اس کو خط لکھوں	I may write a letter to him today.
2. Sháyad woh mujh sē kal milē. شاید وہ مجھ سے کل ملے	He might see me tomorrow.
3. Sháyad áp parsoñ London jaēñ. شاید آپ پرسوں لندن جائیں	You might go to London day after tomorrow.

53

Aorist is also used in the sense of polite imperative:

Urdu	English

1. Abhi jaēň aur kitab laēň.   Please, go just now and bring
   ابھی جائیں اور کتاب لائیں   the book.

2. Áp ziadá neh sochēň.   Please, do not think too much.
   آپ زیادہ نہ سوچیں

Aorist is also used in conditional tenses. A conditional sentence has two clauses: the antecedent clause containing the condition; and the consequent clause. In Urdu antecedent clause begins with 'agar' (اگر) which means 'if', or 'jab' (جب), meaning 'when'. The consequent clause begins with 'to' (تو), instead of a comma in English 'To' (تو) means 'then'. Although this rule is applicable to making conditional tenses of any type (*i.e.,* past, present and future) yet for the sake of continuity of the above discussion, the examples given below are related to Aorist conditional only:

1. Jab áp Islamabad jáēň to Faisal masjid zaroor dēkhēň.
   جب آپ اسلام آباد جائیں تو فیصل مسجد ضرور دیکھیں
2. Agar tum jald thak jáo to foran árám karo.
   اگر تم جلد تھک جاؤ تو فوراً آرام کرو
3. Agar tum Karachi jáo to Lahore ko bhool jáo.
   اگر تم کراچی جاؤ تو لاہور کو بھول جاؤ
4. Jab máň New York jáooň to áp mujh sē zaroor milēň.
   جب میں نیویارک جاؤں تو آپ مجھ سے ضرور ملیں
5. Agar máň paṛhooň to imtehan páss kar looň.
   اگر میں پڑھوں تو امتحان پاس کروں

XIV

Future Tense

Add 'gá' (گا), 'gē' (گے) and 'gi' (گی) to the aorist tense of a verb according to the gender and number of the subject, and you get the future tense, as shown by the following table:

Subject	Aorist	Future Tense
Woh (mas. - sing.)	kháē کھائے	Kháē + gá = kháēgá کھائے گا
Woh (mas. - plu.)	kháēṅ کھائیں	kháēṅ + gē = kháēṅgē کھائیں گے
Áp (mas. - plu.)	kháēṅ کھائیں	kháēṅ + gē = kháēṅgē کھائیں گے
Ham (mas. - plu.)	kháēṅ کھائیں	kháēṅ + gē = kháēṅgē کھائیں گے
Máṅ (mas. - sing.)	kháooṅ کھاؤں	kháooṅ + gá = kháooṅgá کھاؤں گا
Tum (mas. - sing. & plu.)	kháo کھاؤ	kháo + gē = kháogē کھاؤ گے

Use 'gi' (گی) in case of female subjects, both for singular and plural, in place of 'gá' (گا) and 'gē' (گے), which are used for singular and plural, respectively.

EXERCISE

1. Mērá bháei kamrē mēṅ soē gá. — میرا بھائی کمرے میں سوئے گا
2. Kal saṛak par bohat bheeṛ ho gi. — کل سڑک پر بہت بھیڑ ہوگی۔
3. Kiá áp aglē sál Pakistan áēṅ gē? — کیا آپ اگلے سال پاکستان آئیں گے؟
4. Ahista chalo warná geelē farsh par gir jáo gē. — آہستہ چلو ورنہ گیلے فرش پر گر جاؤ گے
5. Ham kal bágh mēṅ sar kareṅ gē. — ہم کل باغ میں سیر کریں گے
6. Kutta tēz daurē gá aur gēnd ko pakṛ lēgá. — کتا تیز دوڑے گا اور گیند کو پکڑ لے گا
7. Ham sárá din car chaláēṅ gē. — ہم سارا دن کار چلائیں گے
8. Áp kal subah dēr sē utheṅ gē magar máṅ jaldi uthooṅ gá. — آپ کل صبح دیر سے اٹھیں گے مگر میں جلدی اٹھوں گا
9. Billi sárá doodh pi jáē gi. — بلی سارا دودھ پی جائے گی
10. Áurteṅ ŕát ko jald so jáēṅ gi. — عورتیں رات کو جلد سو جائیں گی
11. Kiá tum parsoṅ daftar naheeṅ jáo gē? — کیا تم پرسوں دفتر نہیں جاؤ گے؟

12. Ham ab T.V. kabhi naheeṅ dekheṅ gē. ہم اب ٹی وی کبھی نہیں دیکھیں گے

13. Ustád sabaq parháeṅ gē aur talib ilm prheṅ gē. استاد سبق پڑھائیں گے اور طالب علم پڑھیں گے

14. Dukándar kal dukán naheeṅ kholē gá. دوکاندار کل دوکان نہیں کھولے گا

15. Kal college mēṅ chutti ho gi aur parsoṅ phir college khulē gá. کل کالج میں چھٹی ہوگی اور پرسوں پھر کالج کھلے گا

XV
Conditional Future Tense

In English, the antecedent clause of a future tense is always in present tense but the consequent clause is in future tense. In Urdu, on the contrary, both the clauses of a conditional sentence are in future tense, as under:

1. Agar tum mērē ghar áo gē to fáēdē mēṅ raho gē. اگر تم میرے گھر آؤ گے تو فائدے میں رہو گے

2. Jab sooraj niklē gá to māṅ uthooṅ gá. جب سورج نکلے گا تو میں اٹھوں گا

3. Agar māṅ ziádá khāná kháooṅ gá to beemár ho jáooṅ gá. اگر میں زیادہ کھانا کھاؤں گا تو بیمار ہو جاؤں گا

4. Agar tum seerhi par charho gē to gir jáo gē. اگر تم سیڑھی پر چڑھو گے تو گر جاؤ گے

5. Jab mali áyē gá to darakt kát dē gá. جب مالی آئے گا تو درخت کاٹ دے گا

XVI
"Hogá" Expressing Doubt

The present tense of "honá" (ہونا) is hā (ہے), the conjugation of which we have already learnt its future tense is 'hogá' (ہوگا), but it expresses doubt. The action does not take place in future. It is used in the sense of "would be" or "might be". The other declensions of "hogá" are as under:

Subject	Declension
1. Woh (mas. - plu.)	Hoṅ gē ہوں گے
2. Woh (fem. - plu.)	Hoṅ gi ہوں گی
3. Tum (mas. - sing. & plu.)	Ho gē ہو گے

4. Tum (fem. - sing. & plu.)   Ho gi   ہو گی

5. Ap/Ham (mas. - sing. & plu.)   Hoň gē   ہوں گے

6. Ap/Ham (fem. - sing. & plu.)   Hoň gi   ہوں گی

Example: Woh áp kē dost hoň gē. (They might be your friends.)

وہ آپ کے دوست ہوں گے

EXERCISE

1. Áp ka naukar chor ho gá.   آپ کا نوکر چور ہو گا
2. Meri beevi is waqt ghar mēň ho gi.   میری بیوی اس وقت گھر میں ہو گی
3. Merá dost áj daftar mēň ho gá.   میرا دوست آج دفتر میں ہو گا
4. Tum kal kaháň ho gē.   تم کل کہاں ہو گے
5. Woh áp kē bháee hoň gē.   وہ آپ کے بھائی ہوں گے

A state of perpetual daubt is expressed as under:

1. Woh har roz daftar játá ho gá.   وہ ہر روز دفتر جاتا ہو گا
2. Áp imtēhan ki tiyári kartē hoň gē.   آپ امتحان کی تیاری کرتے ہوں گے
3. Larkian har roz sēr karti hoň gi.   لڑکیاں ہر روز سیر کرتی ہوں گی
4. Tum ab bhi kuch nahceň kartē ho gē.   تم اب بھی کچھ نہیں کرتے ہو گے
5. Mäň unko pichlē sál bhi milta hooň gá.   میں ان کو پچھلے سال بھی ملتا ہو نگا

Doubt expressed may sometimes have reference to past:

1. Tum pehlē bhi hahaň áē ho gē.   تم پہلے بھی یہاں آئے ہو گے
2. Mujh sē ghalati huee ho gi.   مجھ سے غلطی ہوئی ہو گی
3. Áurtēň bazár sē áee hoň gi.   عورتیں بازار سے آئی ہوں گی
4. Tum America gaē ho gē.   تم امریکہ گئے ہو گے
5. Áp nē yēh kitáb pehlē bhi parhi ho gi.   آپ نے یہ کتاب پہلے بھی پڑھی ہو گی

XVII
Use of Infinitives in Sentences

Verb are derived from infinitives, but sometimes infinitives themselves are used in sentences along with verbs, for example:

1. I am going *to play*.

2. He went there *to see* his friend.

3. He wants *to take rest*.

In the above sentences 'to play', 'to see', 'to take rest' mean for playing, for seeing, for taking rest, respectively. 'For' in Urdu is 'kēliyē' (کے لیے). Hence 'khelnē kēliyē' (کھیلنے کے لیے) means 'for playing' or 'to play'. 'Kēliyē' behaves like a postposition therefore according to usual rules 'khelná' will change into 'khelnē'.

The following examples explain the use of infinitives in the sentences:

1. Woh sonē kēliyē apnē ghar jáē gá. وہ سونے کے لیے اپنے گھر جائے گا

2. Woh apnē dost sē milnē kēliyē Karachi gayá. وہ اپنے دوست سے ملنے کے لیے کراچی گیا

3. Máñ khelnē kēliyē já rahá hooñ. میں کھیلنے کے لیے جا رہا ہوں

Often we omit 'kēliyē' (کے لیے) as in the following examples:

1. Máñ khelnē já rahá hooñ. میں کھیلنے جا رہا ہوں

2. Ham match dekhnē já rahē háñ. ہم میچ دیکھنے جا رہے ہیں۔

3. Kiá áp merē sath kháná khane jaēñ gē? کیا آپ میرے ساتھ کھانا کھانے جائیں گے

When there is no need of a postposition, infinitive form alone is used without inflection, for example:

1. Jaldi soná aur jaldi uthná achchá há. جلدی سونا اور جلدی اٹھنا اچھا ہے

2. Jhoot bolná buri bát há. جھوٹ بولنا بری بات ہے ۔

3. Kitabēñ parhná meri adat há. کتابیں پڑھنا میری عادت ہے

4. Rishwat lēná aur dēná jurm háñ. رشوت لینا اور دینا جرم ہیں

5. Gáná aur roná kaun naheeñ jántá! گانا اور رونا کون نہیں جانتا

XVIII
Expressing Two Actions in Quick Succession

When two actions occur in quick succession, they are expressed in one compound sentence, instead of two simple sentences, as under:

1. On reaching there, I saw nobody.
2. After a long walk, I felt tired.
3. After eating food, I felt pain in my belly.

In Urdu 'on' or 'after' may be translated as 'kē bád' (کے بعد).
Urdu translation of the above sentences is as under:

1. Waháň pohnchnē kē bád māň nē   وہاں پہنچنے کے بعد میں نے کسی کو نہ دیکھا
   kisiko neh dekhá.
2. Lambi sēr kē bád māň thak gayá.   لمبی سیر کے بعد میں تھک گیا
3. Kháná kē bád mērē pēt meň ḍarḍ uthá.   کھانے کے بعد میرے پیٹ میں درد اُٹھا

The other way to make such compound sentences is that of
suffixing 'kar' (کر), declension of the infinitive 'karná' (کرنا), to
the crude imperative, instead of 'kē bád' (کے بعد), as illustrated
below:

1. Wahan pohanch kar māň ne kisi   وہاں پہنچ کر میں نے کسی کو نہ دیکھا
   ko nēh dekhá.
2. Lambi sēr kar kē māň thak gayá.[1]   لمبی سیر کرکے میں تھک گیا
3. Kháná khá kar mērē pēt meň ḍarḍ uthá.   کھانا کھا کر میرے پیٹ میں درد اُٹھا
4. Waháň já kar áp nē kiá dēkhá.   وہاں جا کر آپ نے کیا دیکھا
5. Jab māň so kar uthá to din nikal áyá thá.   جب میں سو کر اُٹھا تو دن نکل آیا تھا
6. Māň ghar já kar cháē peeooň gá.   میں گھر جا کر چائے پیوں گا
7. Kiá tum lēt kar T.V. dēkho gē?   کیا تم لیٹ کر ٹی وی دیکھو گے؟
8. Ham cháē pi kar khēlēň gē.   ہم چائے پی کر کھیلیں گے
9. Tum lēt kar radio naheeň suno gē.   تم لیٹ کر ریڈیو نہیں سنو گے
10. Māň khará ho kar kháná kháooň gá.   میں کھڑا ہو کر کھانا کھاؤں گا

---

1. The crude imperative of 'karná' (کرنا) is kar (کر).
   Therefore, 'sēr kar kar' (سیر کرکر) is grammatically correct but the
   repetition of 'kar kar' does not sound pleasant to the year so
   second 'kar' has been changed into 'kē' (کے).

XIX

Direct and Indirect Speech

Speech is of two kinds: direct and indirect. He said, "He is going to London," is direct speech. He told me that he was going to London, is its indirect form.

In Urdu, unlike English, the method of converting direct speech into indirect is very simple. Remove inverted commas and put 'keh' (کہ) for "that" in the beginning of the speech and direct form changes into indirect, as illustrated below:

Direct

1. Mērá dost bolá, "tumhárá nám kiá hā?" میرا دوست بولا:"تمہارا نام کیا ہے ؟"

Indirect

Mērá dost bolá keh tumhárá nám kiá hā? میرا دوست بولا کہ تمہارا نام کیا ہے ؟

Direct

2. Ustád nē larkoň ko hukm diyá: استاد نے لڑکوں کو حکم دیا:"فوراً کلاس سے نکل جاؤ"
"fauran class sē nikal jáo."

Indirect

Ustád nē larkoň ko hukm diyá استاد نے لڑکوں کو حکم دیا کہ فوراً کلاس سے نکل جاؤ
keh fauran class sē nikal jáo.

XX

Passive Voice

Active voice expresses the action done by the subject on the verb. The subject, in case of a passive voice, does not act but is acted upon, for example:

Active Voice	*Passive Voice*
1. I read the book.	The book was read by me.
2. Police killed the robber.	The robber was killed by the police.

In Urdu, active voice is changed into passive voice by adding the relevant declensions of the infinitive 'jáná' (جانا), {*i.e.*, 'gayá' (گیا), 'gayē' (گئے), 'gayi' (گئی) and 'gaeeň' (گئیں)} at the end of

60

the sentence, in accordance with the gender and number of the subject.

The following examples illustrate this point:

1. Mujhē library mēṅ kitabēṅ dikháee gaeeṅ. مجھے لائبریری میں کتابیں دکھائی
2. Sipáhi jaṅg mēṅ márá gayá. سپاہی جنگ میں مارا گیا
3. Afsar áj daftar mēṅ naheeṅ dēkhá gayá. افسر آج دفتر میں نہیں دیکھا گیا
4. Ghareeb ádmi ko khaná khiláyá gayá. غریب آدمی کو کھانا کھلایا گیا ۔
5. Ham sē waháṅ khoob kám liyá játá hā. ہم سے وہاں خوب کام لیا جاتا ہے ۔
6. Us ká roná mujh sē naheeṅ dekhá jáyē gá. اُس کا رونا مجھ سے نہیں دیکھا جائیگا ۔
7. Áj hamári team sē achcha naheeṅ khelá gayá. آج ہماری ٹیم سے اچھا نہیں کھیلا گیا
8. Áp sē rát ko árám sē naheeṅ soyá gayá. آپ سے رات کو آرام سے نہیں سویا گیا ۔
9. Mujh sē khat ká jawáb jald naheeṅ diyá játá. مجھ سے خط کا جواب جلدی نہیں دیا جاتا
10. Darakht puráná ho chuká hā isliyē kát diyá jayē gá. درخت پُرانا ہو چکا ہے اسلیے کاٹ دیا جائے گا ۔

XXI
Use of Sakná and Saká
درخت پُرانا ہو چکا ہے اسلیے کاٹ دیا جائے گا ۔

"Can" in English and its equivalent 'sakná' سکنا in Urdu is an auxiliary verb. When the imperative of a verb is prefixed to its various declensions, it intensifies the meaning of permission or approval, as illustrated below:

	English	Urdu	
1.	I can write.	Māṅ likh sakta hooṅ.	میں لکھ سکتا ہوں ۔
2.	You can go.	Tum já saktē ho.	تم جا سکتے ہو ۔
3.	I can run.	Māṅ daur sakta hooṅ.	میں دوڑ سکتا ہوں ۔
4.	He cannot come.	Woh naheeṅ á saktá.	وہ نہیں آ سکتا ۔
5.	We can walk.	Ham chal saktē hāṅ.	ہم چل سکتے ہیں ۔

EXERCISE

1. Áurteṅ zabáneṅ ásáni sē seekh sakti hāṅ. عورتیں زبانیں آسانی سے سیکھ سکتی ہیں ۔

2. Tum har jagá já saktē ho. تم ہر جگہ جا سکتے ہو

3. Mujhē koi naheeň rok saktá. مجھے کوئی نہیں روک سکتا ۔

4. Har shakhs match dekhnē ہر شخص میچ دیکھنے جاسکتا ہے ۔
   já saktá ĥā.

5. Tum bēth naheeň saktē. تم بیٹھ نہیں سکتے ۔

"Saká" (سکا) is the past tense of sakná (سکنا) in Urdu, just as 'could' is the past tense of 'can' in English. In the past form 'saká' (سکا) and sakē (سکے) are used in place of 'saktá' (سکتا) and 'saktē' (سکتے) in the present form.

Examples

1. Mäň rát ko so naheeň saká. میں رات کو سو نہیں سکا ۔

2. Tum khat naheeň likh sakē. تم خط نہیں لکھ سکے ۔

3. Ham kal mushkil sē bus pakar sakē. ہم کل مشکل سے بس پکڑ سکے ۔

4. Kiá áp áj khána khá sakē? کیا آپ آج کھانا کھا سکے ؟

5. Larkē áj football naheeň khēl sakē. لڑکے آج فٹ بال نہیں کھیل سکے

XXII
Action Done Under Compulsion

"I went there" means that I went there on my own. "I had to go there" indicates that I was compelled to go. An action done under compulsion is expressed in Urdu by suffixing the relevant inflection of the infinitive 'parná' (پڑنا) – pará (پڑا), partá (پڑتا), parē gá (پڑے گا) – to the infinitive expressing the action, as illustrated by the following examples:

1. Mujhe daftar jáná pará. مجھے دفتر جانا پڑا ۔

2. Hamēň bási khána khána pará. ہمیں باسی کھانا کھانا پڑا ۔

3. Temhēň roz subh college تمہیں روز صبح کالج جانا پڑتا ہے ۔
   jáná partá ĥā.

4. Thak kar soná partá ĥā. تھک کر سونا پڑتا ہے ۔

5. Imtehán kē liyē parhná partá ĥā. امتحان کے لیے پڑھنا پڑتا ہے ۔

6. Ápko ab Karáchi jáná parē gá. آپ کو اب کراچی جانا پڑے گا ۔

7. Har Insán ko ēk din marná parē gá. ہر انسان کو ایک دن مرنا پڑے گا ۔

62

Use of 'Chahna' and 'Chahiye'

As an auxiliary verb 'chahna' expresses the wish of the agent. Whatever declension of it is suffixed to infinitive form of a verb, it conveys the same meaning.[1]

XXIII

Examples

1. Hameṅ soch kar kám karná chahiyē.   ہمیں سوچ کر کام کرنا چاہیے۔
2. Hameṅ Urdu seekhná chahiyē.   ہمیں اردو سیکھنا چاہیے۔
3. Tumheṅ yēh kitab paṛhná chahiyē.   تمہیں کتاب پڑھنا چاہیے۔
4. Mujhē roti khāná chahiyē.   مجھے روٹی کھانا چاہیے۔
5. Sab logoṅ ko mehnat karna chahiyē.   سب لوگوں کو محنت کرنا چاہیے۔

XXIV

Past, Present and Future Forms of 'Chahna'

Examples

1. Māṅ America jáná chahta hooṅ.   میں امریکہ جاتا چاہتا ہوں۔
2. Kiá tum cháwal khāná chahtē ho?   کیا تم چاول کھانا چاہتے ہو؟
3. Ham is waqt sona chahti hāṅ.   ہم اس وقت سونا چاہتی ہیں۔
4. Tum nē kion jáná chahá?   تم نے کیوں جانا چاہا؟
5. Ham nē din ko soná chahá.   ہم نے دن کو سونا چاہا۔
6. Māṅ nē pankhá chaláná chahá
   magar woh kharáb thá.   میں نے پنکھا چلانا چاہا مگر وہ خراب تھا۔
7. Māṅ dost ko khat likhná chahooṅ gá.   میں دوست کو خط لکھنا چاہوں گا۔
8. Kiá áp árám karná chaheṅ gē?   کیا آپ آرام کرنا چاہیں گے۔
9. Laṛki kitab paṛhná chahē gi.   لڑکی کتاب پڑھنا چاہے گی۔
10. Árteṅ is waqt khelná naheeṅ chaheṅ gi.
    عورتیں اس وقت کھیلنا نہیں چاہیں گی۔

---

1. In Delhi and Lahore, infinitive is also made faminine if the object is feminine; therefore, 'kitab paṛhni chahiyē' etc. is also correct.

Chapter V

SOME MORE GRAMMAR

Degrees of Comparison

In English, there are three degrees of comparison of the adjectives and adverbs, namely positive, comparative and superlative.

Examples

	Positive	Comparative	Superlative
1.	Good	Better	Best
2.	Bad	Worse	Worst
3.	Fast	Faster	Fastest

In Urdu also these degrees of comparison exist. For changing the positive degree into comparative, prefix 'sē' (ے) with it and for getting superlative degree prefix 'sab' (سب) with the comparative degree, as illustrated below:

Positive		Comparative		Superlative	
Achchá	اچھا	sē achchá	سے اچھا	sab sē achchá	سے اچھا
Tēz	تیز	sē tēz	سے تیز	sab sē tēz	سب سے تیز

Examples in Sentences

1. Mērá ghorá áp kē ghorē sē achchá hā.   میرا گھوڑا آپ کے گھوڑے سے اچھا ہے
2. Mērá bará bētá chotē bētē sē láiq hā.   میرا بڑا بیٹا چھوٹے بیٹے سے لائق ہے
3. Behan bháee sē tēz daurti hā.   بہن بھائی سے تیز دوڑتی ہے
4. Yēh sab sē khoobsoorat larki hā.   یہ سب سے خوبصورت لڑکی ہے

Use of Wálá

"Wálá" is a suffix commonly used in Urdu. It means an owner or possessor, as illustrated below:

English	Urdu meaning with 'Wálá'		Finer Urdu expression	
1. Shopkeeper	Dukán wálá	دكان والا	Dukándár	دكاندار
2. Taxi driver	Taxi wálá	ٹيكسی والا	Driver	ڈرايور
3. Husband	Ghar wálá	گھر والا	Kháwind	خاوند
4. Learner	Seekhnē wálá	سيكھنے والا	Shágird	شاگرد
5. Dancing girl	Nachnē wáli	ناچنے والی	Raqqásá	رقاصہ
6. Writer	Likhnē wálá	لكھنے والا	Adeeb	اديب
7. Baker	Roti bēchnē wálá	روٹی بيچنے والا	Nánbáee	نانبائی

Note: It is desirable to use the finer form of the words given above, instead of their expressions with "wálá".

Use of "Áp" and "Apná"

'Áp' (آپ), like myself in English, expresses the commitment of the agent to do a certain thing personally. 'Khud' (خود) may also be used in place of 'áp' (آپ) which has the same meaning, as illustrated below:

1. Máň áp bazár gayá. ميں آپ بازار گيا۔
2. Tum yēh kám khud karo. تم يہ كام خود كرو ۔
3. Tum khud jáo, máň naheeň jáooň gá. تم خود جاؤ ميں نہيں جاؤں گا۔

The word 'apna' (اپنا) is used in place of possessive pronouns, when the agent is the possessor of the thing indicated by the noun following it. The faminine form of 'apná' is 'apni' (اپنی) and the plural form is 'apnē' (اپنے), both for males and females.

Examples

1. Woh mēri kitáb parh rahá hā.
   (He is reading my book.)

   وہ میری کتاب پڑھ رہا ہے ۔

2. Woh apni kitáb parh rahá hā.
   (He is reading his [own] book.)

   وہ اپنی کتاب پڑھ رہا ہے ۔

3. Woh mērē pen sē likh rahá hā.
   (He is writing with my pen.)

   وہ میرے پن سے لکھ رہا ہے ۔

4. Woh apnē pen sē likh rahá hā.
   (He is writing with his [own] pen.)

   وہ اپنے پن سے لکھ رہا ہے ۔

EXERCISE

1. Woh apni gári chalá rahá hā.

   وہ اپنی گاڑی چلا رہا ہے ۔

2. Tum apna jutá polish kar rahē ho.

   تم اپنا جوتا پالش کر رہے ہو ۔

3. Māň apni kaháni suná rahá hooň.

   میں اپنی کہانی سنا رہا ہوں ۔

4. Áp apni ghari kharáb kar rahē hāň.

   آپ اپنی گھڑی خراب کر رہے ہیں ۔

5. Bachchá apni kitáb phár rahá hā.

   بچہ اپنی کتاب پھاڑ رہا ہے ۔

6. Báp apnē bētē ko már rahá hā.

   باپ اپنے بیٹے کو مار رہا ہے ۔

7. Tum apná kam naheeň kar rahē.

   تم اپنا کام نہیں کر رہے ۔

8. Larká apná sabaq yád kartá hā.

   لڑکا اپنا سبق یاد کرتا ہے ۔

9. Larki apná muňh dho rahi hā.

   لڑکی اپنا منہ دھو رہی ہے ۔

10. Ustád apná kot pehn rahá hā.

    استاد اپنا کوٹ پہن رہا ہے ۔

Use of Sá

Sá, si and sē (سے ، سی ، سا) are suffixed in Urdu to an indefinite adjective of quality to express some modification of the meaning. Sá is used for masculine nouns, si for faminine and sē for plural.

Examples

1. Thori si cháe láo.   تھوڑی سی چائے لاؤ
2. Mēz par bohat sē kaghz parē hāǹ.   میز پر بہت سے کاغذ پڑے ہیں
3. Zará sá doodh pi lo.   ذرا سا دودھ پی لو۔

'Sá' also means 'to be similar to', to have likeness of. Sá, in this sense, is an abbreviated form of 'jāsá'.

Examples

1. Áp sá aur koei naheeǹ.   آپ سا اور کوئی نہیں۔
2. Sab nē laṛki ká guláb sá chehra dekhá.   سب نے لڑکی کا گلاب سا چہرہ دیکھا۔

List of Conjunctions

A conjunction is a word that connects sentences, clauses and words. Below is given a list of commonly used conjunctions, in Urdu, along with their equivalents in English:

	Urdu		English
1.	Aur	اور	And
2.	Magar/Lēkin	مگر/لیکن	But
3.	Agar	اگر	If
4.	Jab	جب	When
5.	Agarchē	اگرچہ	Although
6.	To	تو	Then
7.	Chooǹkē	چونکہ	Because
8.	Warná	ورنہ	Otherwise
9.	Yá	یا	Either, or
10.	Kēh	کہ	That
11.	Phir	پھر	Again
12.	Goyá	گویا	As if

List of Interjections

An interjection is a word thrown in to express emotion, *e.g.*, joy or sorrow, etc. The following words are used as interjections in Urdu:

	Urdu		English Equivalent
1.	Háē	ہائے	Alas
2.	Wáh	واہ	How good
3.	Arē	ارے	O!
4.	Afsos	افسوس	How sad
5.	Shábásh	شاباش	Well done
6.	Kash	کاش	Would that

Cardinal Numbers

A numeral is a figure or mark used to express a number as 1, 2, etc. Numbers are of two kinds; cardinal and ordinal. Cardinal numbers express how many, that is 1, 2, 3, etc. Ordinal numbers express order of place among others, *e.g.* 1st, 2nd, 3rd, etc.

We deal with cardinal numbers first. It is not easy to learn them in Urdu. They require rigorous practice for gaining mastery over them, because they are not so systematic as they are in English.

A complete list of cardinal numbers in Urdu, both in words and figures, from one to hundred is given below:

International Symbol	Urdu Symbol	In Figures		International Symbol	Urdu Symbol	In Figures	
1	١	Ek	ایک	4	۴	Chár	چار
2	٢	Do	دو	5	۵	Pánch	پانچ
3	٣	Teen	تین	6	۶	Chē	چھ

68

#		Urdu	#		Urdu
7	۷	Sát سات	38	۳۸	Artees اڑتیس
8	۸	Áth آٹھ	39	۳۹	Untálees انتالیس
9	۹	Nau نو	40	۴۰	Chálees چالیس
10	۱۰	Das دس	41	۴۱	Iktálees اکتالیس
11	۱۱	Giárá گیارہ	42	۴۲	Biálees بیالیس
12	۱۲	Bárá بارہ	43	۴۳	Táňtálees تینتالیس
13	۱۳	Tērá تیرہ	44	۴۴	Chawálees چوالیس
14	۱۴	Chaudá چودہ	45	۴۵	Páňtálees پینتالیس
15	۱۵	Paňdrá پندرہ	46	۴۶	Chchiálees چھیالیس
16	۱۶	Solá سولہ	47	۴۷	Sáňtalees سینتالیس
17	۱۷	Satrá سترہ	48	۴۸	Artálees اڑتالیس
18	۱۸	Athárá اٹھارہ	49	۴۹	Unchás انچاس
19	۱۹	Unnees اُنیس	50	۵۰	Pachchás پچاس
20	۲۰	Bees بیس	51	۵۱	Ikawan اکاون
21	۲۱	Ikkees اکیس	52	۵۲	Bawan باون
22	۲۲	Báees بائیس	53	۵۳	Trapan ترپین
23	۲۳	Tēees تیئیس	54	۵۴	Chawan چون
24	۲۴	Chaubees چوبیس	55	۵۵	Pachpan پچپن
25	۲۵	Pachchees پچیس	56	۵۶	Chappan چھپن
26	۲۶	Chchabbees چھبیس	57	۵۷	Satawan ستاون
27	۲۷	Satáees ستائیس	58	۵۸	Athawan اٹھاون
28	۲۸	Atháees اٹھائیس	59	۵۹	Unsath انسٹھ
29	۲۹	Untees اُنتیس	60	۶۰	Sáth ساٹھ
30	۳۰	Tees تیس	61	۶۱	Iksath اکسٹھ
31	۳۱	Ikattees اکتیس	62	۶۲	Básath باسٹھ
32	۳۲	Battees بتیس	63	۶۳	Trēsath ترسٹھ
33	۳۳	Táňtees تینتیس	64	۶۴	Chauňsath چوسٹھ
34	۳۴	Chauňtees چونتیس	65	۶۵	Páňsath پینسٹھ
35	۳۵	Páňtees پنتیس	66	۶۶	Chiásath چھیاسٹھ
36	۳۶	Chattees چھتیس	67	۶۷	Sarsath سرسٹھ
37	۳۷	Sáňtees سنتیس	68	۶۸	Arsath ارسٹھ

69	٦٩	Unhattar	انہتر	85	٨٥	Pachási	پچاسی
70	٧٠	Sattar	ستر	86	٨٦	**Chiasi**	چھیاسی
71	٧١	Ikhatar	اکتہر	87	٨٧	Satási	ستاسی
72	٧٢	Bahatar	بہتر	88	٨٨	Athási	اٹھاسی
73	٧٣	Tihattar	تہتر	89	٨٩	Nawasi	نواسی
74	٧٤	Chauhattar	چوہتر	90	٩٠	Nawē	نوے
75	٧٥	**Pachattar**	پچھتر	91	٩١	Ikanwē	اکانوے
76	٧٦	Chihattar	چھہتر	92	٩٢	Banwē	بانوے
77	٧٧	Stattar	تہتر	93	٩٣	Tiránwē	ترانوے
78	٧٨	Athattar	اٹھتر	94	٩٤	Chauránwē	چورانوے
79	٧٩	Unási	اناسی	95	٩٥	Pachánwē	پچانوے
80	٨٠	Assi	اسی	96	٩٦	Chchiánwē	چھیانوے
81	٨١	Ikiási	اکیاسی	97	٩٧	Satánwē	ستانوے
82	٨٢	Biási	بیاسی	98	٩٨	Athánwē	اٹھانوے
83	٨٣	Tirási	تراسی	99	٩٩	Ninánwē	ننانوے
84	٨٤	Chaurasi	چوراسی	100	١٠٠	Sau	سو

Thousand Onward

One thousand	1,000	Ek hazár	ایک ہزار
Ten thousand	10,000	Das hazár	دس ہزار
Hundred thousand	100,000	Ek lákh	ایک لاکھ
Ten million	10,000,000	Ek cror	ایک کروڑ

Ordinal Numbers

English	*Urdu*	
First	Pehlá	پہلا
Second	Doosrá	دوسرا
Third	Teesrá	تیسرا
Fourth	Chauthá	چوتھا
Fifth	Pánchwáň	پانچواں
Sixth	Chatá	چھٹا

70

English	Urdu	
Seventh	Sátwáň	ساتواں
Eighth	Athwáň	آٹھواں
Ninth	Nawáň	نواں
Tenth	Daswáň	دسواں

From sátwáň (seventh) onward 'wáň' (واں) is added to every cardinal number for changing it into ordinal number.

Days of the Week

English	*Urdu*	
Friday	Jumá	جمعہ
Saturday	Haftá	ہفتہ
Sunday	Itwár	اتوار
Monday	Peer or Somwar	پیر/سو موار
Tuesday	Mangal	منگل
Wednesday	Budh	بدھ
Thursday	Jumērát	جمعرات

Months of the Year

Solar calendar is as much in use in Pakistan as lunar calendar. The names of the twelve months of the solar calendar, used in Urdu, are basically the same used in English, but they have undergone a little change in pronunciation in Urdu, as shown below:

English	*Urdu*	
January	Janwari	جنوری
February	Farwari	فروری
March	March	مارچ
April	Aprēl	اپریل
May	Máee	مئی

71

June	June	جون
July	July	جولائی
August	Agast	اگست
September	Satambar	ستمبر
October	Actoober	اکتوبر
November	Novamber	نومبر
December	December	دسمبر

Seasons of the Year

English	*Urdu*	
Spring	Bahár	بہار
Summer	Garmi	گرمی
Winter	Sarḍi	سردی
Autumn	Khizáñ	خزاں
Rainy Season	Barsát	برسات

Useful Words and Phrases

ٹھیک ہے
درست ہے } It is all right.

ظاہر ہے — It is obvious.

مجھے یقین ہے — I believe.

مجھے اتفاق ہے — I agree.

مجھے افسوس ہے — I am sorry.

مجھے معاف کیجیے — Excuse me.

72

یہ ممکن نہیں	It is not possible.
میں مصروف ہوں	I am busy.
براہِ کرم مہربانی کر کے	Kindly
کیا آپ بتا سکتے ہیں ؟	Can you tell
بہت شکریہ	Thank you very much.
میں ممنون ہوں میں شکر گزار ہوں	I am obliged
کوئی بات نہیں	No mention, please.
یقیناً	Certainly.

VOCABULARY

Select List of Nouns, Adjectives, etc.

انسان	آج
انگلینڈ	آج کل
باپ	آدمی
بازار	آرام
بازو	آگ
باسی	آنکھ
باغ	آواز
باہر	آہستہ
بچہ	اچھا
بدصورت	اخبار
بڑا	ادیب
بڑھیا	اردو
بس	استاد
بوتل	استانی
بہن	اگلا
بیلا	الماری
بیمار	امتحان
بیوی	امریکہ
بھائی	اندھا
ٹولی	بھدیر
ٹونی	پاکستان
ٹی۔وی	پالش
ٹھنڈا	پانی

74

جان	پچھلا
جرم	پرانا
حلدی	پرسوں
جناب	مڑویا
جنگ	پن
جوتا	پنسل
جیب	پنکھا
جھوٹ	پودا
چاقو	پریس
چارپائی	پھل
چابی	پھول
چاول	تالا
چائے	تحفہ
چروایا	تقریر
چمچ	تیاری
چور	تیز
دھوبی	چینی
ڈاکخانہ	چھری
ڈاکیہ	چھوٹا
رات	خراب
رسالہ	خط
رشوت	خوبصورت
رقاصہ	خوشی
روبہ	درخت
روٹی	درد
روشنی	درزی
سال	دروازہ

دریا	سانپ
دفتر	سبز
دفعہ	سیٹی
دکان	سپاہی
دکاندار	سرخ
دلچسپ	سکول
دودھ	سگرٹ
دور	سورج
دوست	سیر
سیڑھی	کتاب
شاگرد	کراچی
تصویر	کرسی
شیشہ	کرکٹ
صابن	چیڑا
صندوق	کتنا
طالب علم	کل
عورت	کلاس
غریب	کند
غلطی	کندھا
فرش	کوٹ
فائدہ	کہانی
فٹ بال	کھانا
فرش	کھڑکی
تعلیم	گاڑی
قمیض	گانا
کاپی	گرم
کاغذ	گرمیاں

76

گلاس	کالج
گلی	گندہ
مکان	گھر
ملازمت	گھڑی
موٹا	گھنٹہ
میچ	گھوڑا
میدان	گھوڑی
مینر	لاہور
باقشدہ	لائق
نام	لڑکا
نوکر	لڑکی
نوکرانی	لکڑی
نیا	لمبا
وجہ	لنگڑا
وقت	لوگ
ہاتھ	مالک
ہاتھی	مال
ہمسایہ	ماں
سہول	مچھر
پ	مسجد
	مشکل

Select list of Infinitives

ٹوٹنا   اڑانا

جانا   آرام کرنا

جاگنا   آنا

جاننا   اٹھنا

چلنا   تلانا

چھپانا   بچنا

چھوڑنا   بٹھانا

ختم کرنا   بولنا

خریدنا   بہنا

دھونا   بیچنا

دوڑنا   بیٹھنا

دیکھنا   کھونا

دنیا   کھینا

ڈالنا   پڑھانا

رکھنا   پڑھنا

رونا   پکارنا

سنانا   پہننا

سوچنا   پینا

سونا   تھکنا

مرنا   سیرکرنا

ملانا   سیکھنا

ملنا   کام کرنا

نکالنا   کاٹنا

نکلنا   کرنا

ہونا   کہنا

78

لگنا

لیٹنا

مانگنا

محنت کرنا

مدد کرنا

کھانا

کھولنا

کھیلنا

گانا

گرنا

گذرنا

لانا

لکھنا

EXERCISES

تعارف

ایک شخص جس کا نام راشد ہے، کراچی سے آیا ہے۔ وہ لاہور کے ایک دفتر میں جاتا ہے جہاں وہ ایک افسر سے ملنا چاہتا ہے۔ جس کا نام یوسف ہے

راشد : (دفتر کے چپراسی سے) کیا یوسف صاحب دفتر میں تشریف رکھتے ہیں؟

چپراسی : جی ہاں۔

راشد : مہربانی کرکے میرا کارڈ انہیں دیجئے۔

(چپراسی کارڈ کے ساتھ اندر جاتا ہے اور کچھ دیر میں واپس آتا ہے)

چپراسی : یوسف صاحب آپ کا انتظار کر رہے ہیں۔ اندر تشریف لے جائیے۔

(راشد کمرے میں داخل ہوتا ہے)

راشد : (یوسف سے) : السلام علیکم

یوسف : وعلیکم السلام

راشد : میرا نام راشد ہے اور میں کراچی سے آیا ہوں۔ میں وہاں ایک کمپنی میں کام کرتا ہوں۔

یوسف : میں آپ کے کس کام آ سکتا ہوں؟

راشد : میری کمپنی نے مجھے آپ کے پاس ایک دفتری کام سے بھیجا ہے۔

(راشد انہیں معاملے کی تفصیل بتاتا ہے)

یوسف : یہ چند دن میں ہو جائے گا۔

راشد : میں آپ کا ممنون ہوں گا۔ اب میں اجازت چاہتا ہوں۔ خدا حافظ۔

یوسف : خدا حافظ۔

ریل گاڑی کا سفر

مسافر (ٹیکسی ڈرائیور سے) میں سٹیشن پر جانا چاہتا ہوں ۔

ڈرائیور : ٹھیک ہے، میں لے جاؤں گا۔

مسافر : سٹیشن، یہاں سے کتنا دور ہے ؟

ڈرائیور : زیادہ دور نہیں ہے، صرف چھ کلو میٹر ہے۔

مسافر : (سٹیشن پر پہنچنے کے بعد)
ٹکٹ گھر کہاں ہے ؟

ڈرائیور : بالکل سامنے ہے ۔

مسافر : (ٹکٹ گھر کی کھڑکی پر پہنچ کر)
ملتان کا ایک ٹکٹ دیجیے ۔

بابو : کس درجے کا ٹکٹ چاہیے ؟

مسافر : ایئر کنڈیشنڈ کا
کتنے روپے ؟

بابو : دو سو روپے

مسافر : (معلومات کی کھڑکی پر پہنچ کر)
کیا ملتان کو جانے والی گاڑی لیٹ ہے (دیر سے آ رہی ہے)

بابو : جی نہیں ٹھیک وقت پر آئے گی۔

مسافر : یہ گاڑی کتنی دیر میں ملتان پہنچ جاتی ہے ۔

بابو : پانچ گھنٹوں میں۔

ہوائی جہاز پر

مسافر: کیا امریکہ کے لیے ٹکٹ مل جائے گا؟

کلرک: آپ کب جانا چاہتے ہیں؟

مسافر: میں ۳ مارچ کو جانا چاہتا ہوں

کلرک: تین مارچ کو ۵ بجے شام طیارہ امریکہ جاتا ہے۔

مسافر: ٹھیک ہے ایک ٹکٹ دے دیجیئے۔

کلرک: یہ ٹکٹ صرف یک طرفہ درکار ہے یا آمدورفت کا؟

مسافر: یک طرفہ

کلرک: کیا آپ سگریٹ پیتے ہیں؟

مسافر: جی نہیں۔ مجھے کھڑکی کے ساتھ والی نشست دیجیئے

کلرک: مل جائے گی۔

ویٹر: (مسافر سے) آپ کیا پئیں گے۔

مسافر: کیا کچھ مل جائے گا؟

ویٹر: لیمن، کوکا کولا، چائے، کافی

مسافر: کافی ٹھیک رہے گی۔

ویٹر: بہتر

مسافر: جہاز کتنی دیر میں روانہ ہوگا اور نیویارک کے ہوائی اڈے پر کب اترے گا؟

ویٹر: پندرہ منٹ میں جہاز روانہ ہو جائے گا۔ نیویارک اٹھارہ گھنٹوں میں پہنچے گا۔

84

شہر میں

مسافر : (ٹیکسی ڈرائیور سے) مجھے کسی اوسط درجے کے ہوٹل میں لے چلو ۔

ڈرائیور : ٹھیک ہے ۔ گاڑی میں بیٹھ جائیے ۔

مسافر : کرایہ کیا ہوگا؟

ڈرائیور : میٹر کرایہ بتائے گا ۔ ایک کلومیٹر کے پانچ روپے لگتے ہیں ۔

مسافر : (د ہوٹل میں پہنچ کر کلرک سے)
مجھے ایک کمرہ چاہیے ۔

کلرک : تیسری ہی منزل پر کمرہ نمبر تین سو دس خالی ہے ۔

مسافر : بیرا ! سامان اوپر لے چلو

(آرام کرنے کے بعد مسافر شہر کی سیر کرنا چاہتا ہے)

(کلرک سے)

مسافر : میں شہر کے اہم مقامات دیکھنا چاہتا ہوں ۔ کیا آپ ٹیکسی منگوا سکتے ہیں ؟

کلرک : کیوں نہیں، ہوٹل کی اپنی ٹیکسیاں ہیں ۔ آپ کہاں جائیں گے ؟

مسافر : میں پہلے راول ڈیم دیکھنا چاہتا ہوں ۔ وہاں سے اسلام آباد جاؤں گا ۔ وہاں فیصل مسجد دیکھوں گا ۔

کلرک : میں ڈرائیور کو بلا کر سمجھا دیتا ہوں ۔

مسافر : ٹھیک ہے ، شکریہ

مکالمہ - ۱

رحیم : ڈاکٹر صاحب! میری بچی کی طبیعت خراب ہے۔

ڈاکٹر : بچی کو اس پلنگ پر لٹا دیجئے

رحیم : کل سے اس کی طبیعت خراب ہے۔

ڈاکٹر : کل اس نے کیا کھایا تھا؟

رحیم : کل ہم ایک دعوت میں گئے تھے، شاید اس نے وہاں خراب کھانا کھایا۔

ڈاکٹر : کیا پیٹ میں درد ہے؟

رحیم : جی ہاں

ڈاکٹر : پریشانی کی کوئی بات نہیں، میں نے اچھی طرح دیکھ لیا ہے۔ میں دوا لکھ دیتا ہوں۔ بازار سے منگوا لیجئے اور ہر چار گھنٹے کے بعد دو گولیاں پانی کے ساتھ دیجئے۔ کل تک ٹھیک ہو جائے گی۔

مکالمہ ۔ ۲

ڈاکٹر : بیگم صاحبہ! پریشانی کی کوئی بات نہیں، میں نے اچھی طرح معائنہ کر لیا ہے ۔صرف تھکان کی
وجہ سے حرارت ہو گئی ہے ۔غالباً ان دنوں آپ کے شوہر بہت زیادہ کام کرتے ہیں ۔

بیوی : بیسوں مرتبہ کہہ چکی ہوں، اتنا کام نہ کیا کرو ۔صحت سے ہاتھ دھو بیٹھو گے مگر خاک اثر نہیں ہوتا

ڈاکٹر : میں نے اچھی طرح تاکید کر دی ہے کہ دل بھر خاموش بیٹھے رہیں ۔

بیوی : دوا کس کس وقت دینی ہے ؟

ڈاکٹر : دوا کی ضرورت نہیں ، آپ صرف ان کے آرام کا خیال رکھئے ۔مریض کے کمرے میں شور و غل
بالکل نہیں ہونا چاہیے ۔

بیوی : آپ اطمینان رکھیں ۔

(ڈاکٹر جاتا ہے)

بیوی (شوہر سے) میں نے کہا ۔ سو گئے کیا ؟

شوہر : یونہی چپکا پڑا ہوا تھا ۔

بیوی : ڈاکٹر صاحب سخت تاکید کر گئے ہیں کہ آپ بات نہ کریں

میاں : ہوں

بیوی : کیا بدن ٹوٹ رہا ہے ؟ کہو تو دبا دوں ؟

شوہر : ہوں

بیوی : کیا زیادہ درد محسوس ہو رہا ہے ؟

میاں : ہوں

بیوی : آپ کیا پئیں گے ؟ نارنجی کا رس ، یخنی یا ساگودانہ ؟

میاں : ساگودانہ

بیوی : اس سے کیا بنے گا ؟ یخنی پی لیجیے ۔مقوی چیز ہے ۔

87

پاکستان

پاکستان ۱۴ اگست ۱۹۴۷ء کو قائم ہوا ۔ اب پاکستان چار صوبوں پر مشتمل ہے اور اس کی آبادی قریباً دس کروڑ ہے ۔ آبادی کے لحاظ سے پنجاب سب سے بڑا صوبہ ہے ، پھر سندھ اس کے بعد سرحدی صوبہ اور سب سے کم آبادی بلوچستان میں ہے حالانکہ رقبے کے لحاظ سے یہی سب سے بڑا صوبہ ہے ۔ پاکستان کے یہ چاروں صوبے اپنی اپنی جگہ بڑے اہم ہیں ۔ پنجاب اور سندھ میں گندم ، چاول ، کپاس ، گنا اور مکئی کی کاشت ہوتی ہے جس سے پاکستان کو قیمتی زرمبادلہ حاصل ہوتا ہے اور ملکی ضرورتیں بھی پوری ہوتی ہیں ۔ پاکستان کا سب سے بڑا شہر کراچی ہے جو سندھ میں واقع ہے ۔ یہ بہت بڑا صنعتی اور تجارتی مرکز ہونے کے علاوہ ایک بین الاقوامی ہوائی اڈا اور قدرتی بندرگاہ ہے ۔ سرحدی صوبے کا بیشتر علاقہ پہاڑی ہے ۔ اس کا سب سے بڑا شہر پشاور ہے ۔

بلوچستان معدنیات سے مالا مال ہے ۔ یہاں کے ایک قصبے سوئی سے قدرتی گیس کا بہت بڑا ذخیرہ دریافت ہوا ہے جو پاکستان بھر میں ایندھن کا کام دے رہا ہے

88

دُنیا کا نقشہ

پاکستان براعظم ایشیا میں واقع ہے ۔ فرانس براعظم یورپ میں ہے اور مصر افریقہ میں ہے ۔

اگر آپ دنیا کا نقشہ دیکھیں تو شمال اوپر کی طرف ہوتا ہے اور جنوب پیچھے کی طرف ۔ مشرق دائیں طرف ہے اور مغرب بائیں طرف ۔

پاکستان کے شمال میں چین واقع ہے ۔ جنوب میں بھارت ۔ مشرق کی طرف بھی بھارت ہے اور مغرب کی طرف ایران ہے ۔ افغانستان شمال مغرب میں واقع ہے ۔ سورج مشرق سے نکلتا ہے اور مغرب میں ڈوبتا ہے ۔ قطبی ستارہ شمال میں ہوتا ہے ۔ دنیا میں جنوب کی طرف بڑے بڑے سمندر واقع ہیں

89

موسم

پاکستان کے بڑے بڑے موسم چار ہیں ۔ سردی، گرمی، بہار، برسات گرمی کا موسم سب سے لمبا ہے ۔ اپریل کے مہینے سے گرمی پڑنا شروع ہوتی ہے اور جولائی تک برابر بڑھتی رہتی ہے جولائی سے بارشوں کا موسم شروع ہو جاتا ہے جو دو ماہ تک جاری رہتا ہے ۔ یہ موسم ختم ہوتا ہے تو سردی شروع ہو جاتی ہے ۔ دسمبر اور جنوری میں شدید سردی پڑتی ہے ۔ فروری سے موسم پھر تبدیل ہو جاتا ہے ۔ یہ موسم بہار کا آغاز ہے ۔ باغوں میں ہر طرف پھول کھل جاتے ہیں ۔ لوگ سیر کے لئے باغوں کا رخ کرنے لگتے ہیں ۔ ہر طرف خوشبو پھیل جاتی ہے آخر مارچ میں یہ موسم بھی ختم ہو جاتا ہے اور دوبارہ گرمی کا طویل ترین موسم شروع ہو جاتا ہے ۔

پاکستان کے پھل

پاکستان میں بہت سے پھل پیدا ہوتے ہیں ۔ پھل صحت کے لئے مفید ہیں ۔
پاکستانی پھلوں میں کیلا ، مالٹا ، کینو ، آم ، سیب ، امرود اور انگور زیادہ پسند کئے جاتے
ہیں ۔ آم بہت میٹھا اور لذیذ ہوتا ہے ۔ سیب صحت کے لئے بہت مفید ہے ۔ مالٹا اور کینو
کی پیداوار پاکستان میں بہت بڑھ گئی ہے ۔

خشک پھل سردیوں میں پسند کئے جاتے ہیں ۔ مونگ پھلی ، چلغوزہ ، اخروٹ اور بادام
خشک پھل ہیں ۔ یہ خشک پھل پاکستان میں بنتے ہیں مگر دوسرے پھل سکتے ہیں ۔

ڈاک خانہ

ڈاک خانہ پاکستان کے ہر شہر اور قصبے میں موجود ہے ۔ ہم ڈاک خانے سے خط ،
لفافے اور ٹکٹیں خریدتے ہیں ۔ منی آرڈر بھی ڈاک خانے سے تقسیم ہوتے ہیں ۔
ہم خط لکھ کر سرخ رنگ کے لیٹر بکس میں ڈال دیتے ہیں ڈاکیہ مقررہ وقت پر یہ بکس کھولتا
ہے اور تمام خط ایک تھیلے میں ڈال کر لے جاتا ہے ۔ اس طرح سارے شہر کے خط بڑے
ڈاک خانے میں جمع ہو جاتے ہیں جہاں انہیں الگ الگ کر کے بذریعہ ریل یا جہاز مختلف علاقوں
کی طرف روانہ کر دیا جاتا ہے ۔
اگر ہمیں کسی کو جلدی پیغام بھیجنا ہو تو تار کے ذریعے بھیجتے ہیں ۔

لاہور

لاہور پاکستان کا ایک بڑا شہر ہے یہ بہت پرانا اور تاریخی شہر ہے ۔ اس کو آباد ہوئے صدیاں گزر چکی ہیں یہ دریائے راوی کے کنارے واقع ہے ۔ لاہور صوبہ پنجاب کا صدر مقام صوبائی حکومت کے تمام دفاتر یہیں ہیں ۔

یہ شہر صدیوں سے صوبے کا صدر مقام چلا آتا ہے مختلف بادشاہوں نے یہاں بہت سی عمارتیں اور سیر گاہیں بنوائیں ۔ لوگ دور دور سے ان عمارتوں اور سیر گاہوں کو دیکھنے آتے ہیں ۔

لاہور کے قابل دید مقامات یہ ہیں عجائب گھر ، چڑیا گھر ، باغ جناح ، شالیمار باغ ، مینار پاکستان ، بادشاہی مسجد اور علامہ اقبال کا مزار

93

گاؤں کا سکول

میں اپنے گاؤں سے دور ایک ہائی سکول میں پڑھتا ہوں اور سکول کے ہاسٹل میں رہتا ہوں۔ ہاسٹل میں مختلف دیہات کے چالیس لڑکے رہتے ہیں۔ ہاسٹل میں ایک استاد طلبہ کی نگرانی کے لئے مغرب میں فجر کی اذان ہوتے ہی سب لڑکے جاگتے ہیں وضو کرکے نماز پڑھتے ہیں۔ کچھ لڑکے سیر کرتے ہیں۔ کچھ دیر کے بعد سب لڑکے ایک بڑے کمرے میں اکٹھے ہوکر ناشتہ کرتے ہیں ناشتہ کرنے کے بعد کپڑے تبدیل کرتے ہیں اور بستہ تیار کرکے سکول چلے جاتے ہیں سکول کی عمارت ہاسٹل کے ہاں کلی ساتھ ہے۔ سکول میں دوپہر تک پڑھائی ہوتی ہے چھٹی کے بعد ہم پھر ہاسٹل آجاتے ہیں۔ کھانا کھانے کے بعد کچھ دوپہر تک آرام کرتے ہیں پھر چند لڑکے سکول کے میدان میں فٹ بال کھیلنے چلے جاتے ہیں۔ شام کو واپس آکر پھر اکٹھے کھانا کھاتے ہیں اور اس کے بعد پڑھائی کا وقت شروع ہو جاتا ہے۔

کھیل کی اہمیّت

ایک نہ ایک وقت کھیلنا بھی ضرور چاہیئے اس سے دل خوش ہوتا ہے اور بدن میں چستی آتی ہے ۔

وہ دیکھو لڑکے میدان میں کھیل رہے ہیں ۔ وہ کبھی اچھلتے ہیں، اور کبھی دوڑتے ہیں ۔ گیند بلا کھیل رہے ہیں ۔ ایک لڑکا بڑا چست ہے مگر دوسرا سست معلوم ہوتا ہے ۔ ایک لڑکا دوڑتے ہوئے گر پڑا ۔ اسے چوٹ نہیں لگی ۔ اس لئے تھوڑی دیر میں اٹھ کر پھر دوڑنے لگے گا ۔

کھیلنا ضروری ہے مگر سارا دن کھیلتے رہنا بھی اچھا نہیں جو لڑکے دن بھر کھیلتے رہتے ہیں وہ استاد کو سبق نہیں سنا سکتے اور امتحان میں فیل ہو جاتے ہیں ۔

چاقو

میرا چاقو دیکھو ۔ یہ فولاد کا بنا ہوا ہے ۔ میں نے اسے دس روپے میں خریدا ہے ۔ اس سے میں پھل کاٹتا ہوں ۔ یہ بہت تیز ہے ۔ اس پر انگلی نہ پھیرو ، انگلی کٹ سکتی ہے ۔ پانی میں نہ گراؤ زنگ لگ جائے گا ۔ اگر بند پڑا رہا تو خراب ہو جائے گا بچے کے ہاتھ میں چاقو دینا خطرناک ہو سکتا ہے سے چاقو سے پھلوں کا چھلکا الگ کیا جاتا ہے اور سبزیاں بنائی جاتی ہیں اگر چاقو سے لکڑی یا کوئی سخت چیز کاٹی جائے تو یہ کند ہو جاتا ہے

96

پالتو جانور

کتا، بلی اور مرغی پالتو جانور ہیں ۔ یہ دنیا کے ہر ملک میں پائے جاتے ہیں ۔ کتا وفادار جانور ہے
وہ اپنے مالک سے پیار کرتا ہے اور گھروں کی حفاظت بھی کرتا ہے ۔ بلی گھروں میں رہتی ہے ۔
یہ دودھ بڑے شوق سے پیتی ہے ۔ چوہوں کی دشمن ہے ۔ چوہے اسے دیکھ کر بھاگ
جاتے ہیں ۔ مرغی انڈے دیتی ہے ۔ اس کا گوشت بھی کھایا جاتا ہے ۔ اب پاکستان میں
بہت سے مرغی خانے (پولٹری فارم) کھل گئے ہیں ۔ مرغی کا گوشت اور انڈے لذیذ اور
طاقت ور ہوتے ہیں ۔

گائے اور بھینس

گائے دودھ دیتی ہے ۔ بھینس بھی دودھ دیتی ہے ۔ لوگ گائے اور بھینس کا دودھ
شوق سے پیتے ہیں ۔ دودھ دینے والے جانوروں میں اونٹنی ، بکری اور بھیڑ بھی شامل ہیں
لیکن ان کا دودھ خوش ذائقہ نہیں ہوتا ۔ بھینس کا دودھ گاڑھا اور نرسے دار ہوتا ہے ۔ گائے
کا دودھ پیلا ہوتا ہے ۔ بھینس کالی اور کبھی کبھی بھوری ہوتی ہے ۔ گائے کے مختلف رنگ ہوتے
ہیں ۔ دودھ سے مکھن ، گھی اور دہی بنتا ہے ۔ دودھ سے مٹھائیاں بھی تیار ہوتی ہیں ۔

چند مفید جانور

گھوڑا، بیل، گدھا اور اونٹ مفید جانور ہیں یہ وزن اٹھاتے ہیں۔ انھیں گاڑیوں میں جوت کر چلایا جاتا ہے۔ بیل پاکستان میں ہل بھی چلاتے ہیں۔

گھوڑا سواری کے کام آتا ہے اور اس پر بوجھ بھی لادتے ہیں۔ گدھا غریب جانور ہے معمولی خوراک کھا کر بھی گذارا کر لیتا ہے۔ ہر قسم کا بوجھ اٹھانے کے کام آتا ہے اونٹ کو صحرا کا جہاز کہتے ہیں۔ ریت میں بوجھ اٹھا کر چلنا اسی کا کام ہے۔

ہزاروں سال پہلے انسان نے ان جانوروں سدھایا اور اُس وقت سے اب تک دُنیا کی ترقی کے لیے استعمال کیا۔

کھانا کھانے کے آداب

کھانا کھانے کے مخصوص آداب ہیں ۔ ان کا خیال رکھنا چاہیئے ۔ کھانا کھانے سے پہلے ہاتھ منہ دھونا چاہیئے ۔ چھوٹے چھوٹے لقمے کھانے چاہیں ۔ خیال رکھنا چاہیئے کہ لباس پر سالن نہ گرے ۔ کھانا اچھی طرح چبا کر کھانا چاہیئے ۔ کھانا بھوک سے کچھ کم کھانا چاہیئے ۔ بھوک سے زیادہ تو بالکل نہیں کھانا چاہیئے ۔ تیز رفتاری سے کھانا مضر ہے ۔ کھانا آہستہ آہستہ دانتوں سے چبانا چاہیئے تاکہ آواز نہ نکلے ۔ کھانا کھانے کے بعد ہاتھ دھونے اور دانت صاف کرنے چاہئیں ۔

100

ماں اور بیٹی

فوزیہ کی امی باورچی خانے میں کھانا پکا رہی ہے ۔ کھانا تیار ہو جائے گا تو سب مل کر کھائیں گے ۔ ننھی فوزیہ اپنے کمرے میں بیٹھی ہے اس کے ہاتھ میں پنسل ہے ۔ میز پر ایک موٹا سا کاغذ پڑا ہے اور وہ پنسل سے کاغذ پر تصویر بنا رہی ہے ۔

امی نے باورچی خانے سے آکر فوزیہ سے پوچھا ۔ فوزیہ تم کیا کر رہی ہو۔ فوزیہ نے جواب دیا ۔ امی جان میں پھلوں کی ٹوکری کی تصویر بنا رہی ہوں ۔ دیکھئے کیلے ، مالٹے ، سیب اور آم کتنے اچھے بنے ہیں ۔ ان میں مختلف رنگ بھی بھر دیے ہیں تاکہ تصویر اصلی پھلوں جیسی نظر آئے ۔

101

سورج

سورج نکلتا ہے تو اندھیرا غائب ہو جاتا ہے ہر طرف روشنی پھیل جاتی ہے ۔ لوگ اپنے اپنے کام میں مصروف ہو جاتے ہیں ۔

دیکھو اکوئی دفتر جا رہا ہے کسی کارخانے کی طرف ہے ۔ بچے سکول جا رہے ہیں اگر سورج نہ ہو تو دنیا میں زندگی ختم ہو جائے سورج کی گرمی سے پھول کھلتے ہیں درخت اور پودے بڑھتے ہیں ۔ ان پر پھل لگتے ہیں ۔ گندم ، چاول اور دوسرے اناج گرمی سے پکتے ہیں ۔ سورج کی شعاعیں بیماریوں کے جراثیم کو مار ڈالتی ہیں ۔ سردیوں میں دھوپ میں بیٹھا اچھا لگتا ہے ۔

سپاہی کی موت

بہادر سپاہی کو میدانِ جنگ سے اٹھا کر ہسپتال میں لائے اس کے جسم کے ہر حصے پر زخموں کے نشان تھے۔ ایک بازو گولہ لگنے سے بالکل اڑ گیا تھا۔ دائیں ٹانگ کا نچلا حصہ بالکل غائب تھا۔ بائیں آنکھ جاتی رہی تھی۔ یہ سمجھ کر کہ وہ مرنے کے قریب ہے اس کی بیوی کو فوراً تار دیا گیا۔ وہ بدقسمت عورت دوسرے دن ہسپتال میں پہنچ گئی جب اس نے خاوند کے مرنے کی خبر سنی تو اس نے زور سے چیخ ماری اور وہ گر پڑی۔

103

پاکستان میں اُردو

آپ اردو زبان تھوڑے سے عرصے میں سیکھ سکتے ہیں ۔ اردو پاکستان کی قومی زبان ہے اور پورے ملک میں رابطے کی زبان بھی ہے ۔ اس لئے اردو سیکھ کر آپ پاکستان میں ہر جگہ آسانی سے گھوم پھر سکیں گے ۔ پچھلے سال ایک غیر ملکی پاکستان میں آیا ۔ وہ اچھی طرح ملک کی سیر نہ کر سکا ۔ شمالی علاقوں میں وہ چند دن رہا لیکن زبان نہ جاننے کی وجہ سے وہاں کے دور دراز علاقوں میں نہ جا سکا ۔ اس لئے تمام غیر ملکی باشندوں کو چاہیئے کہ پاکستان جانے سے پہلے اردو زبان سیکھ لیں ۔

لباس

ہم اپنا جسم ڈھانپنے کے لئے لباس پہنتے ہیں پاکستان میں مردوں کا لباس پتلون کوٹ یا شلوار قمیص ہے ۔ دیہاتوں میں کچھ تو چادر باندھتے ہیں ۔ قمیص کی بجائے کرتہ بھی پہنا جاتا ہے ۔ جو قمیص کے مقابلے میں ڈھیلا ڈھالا لباس ہے اس لئے گرمی میں اچھا لگتا ہے ۔ ہم سردی کے موسم میں گرم لباس پہنتے ہیں اور گرمی کے موسم میں ہلکا لباس ۔ آج کل نائلن وغیرہ کے کپڑوں کا بھی بہت رواج ہے ۔

دھوبی

دھوبی کپڑا دھو رہا ہے ۔ دیکھو دوپہر ہو گئی ہے مگر ابھی تک پانی میں کھڑا ہے ۔ قریب ہی اس کا لڑکا بیٹھا ہے ۔ بیوی گھر سے کھانا لائی ہے ۔ جب اس کا کام ختم ہو گا تو پانی سے باہر نکلے گا اور درخت کے سائے میں بیٹھ کر کھانا کھائے گا ۔ پاس ہی ایک بیل کھڑا ہے اور ایک کتا دھوبی کر رہا ہے ۔

اب بڑے بڑے شہروں میں دھوبیوں کا کام مندا ہو گیا ہے ۔ ڈرائی کلیننگ اور لانڈری کی دکانیں کھل گئی ہیں جہاں بڑی بڑی مشینوں سے کپڑے دھوئے جاتے ہیں بہت سے کپڑے مشین میں ڈال دیئے جاتے ہیں ۔ مشین چلتی ہے تو کپڑوں کا میل نکل جاتا ہے اور صاف کپڑے خشک ہو کر باہر نکال لئے جاتے ہیں پھر گیس یا بجلی کی استری کر کے پیک کھولے جاتے ہیں ۔

درزی

درزی کپڑے سی رہا ہے۔ یہ درزی بڑا کاریگر ہے۔ کپڑا ایسا اچھا کاٹتا اور سیتا ہے کہ بدن پر ٹھیک آجاتا ہے۔ اسی وجہ سے یہ مشہور ہے۔ دکان میں کپڑوں کا ڈھیر لگا رہتا ہے۔ شاگرد بھی بٹھا رکھے ہیں۔ دیکھو شاگرد کپڑے سی رہا ہیں اور درزی قینچی سے کپڑا کاٹ رہا ہے۔ استری پاس رکھی ہے۔ جب کپڑے تیار ہو جاتے ہیں تو مالک کو پہنتا ہے ؟

میاں درزی ! تم کپڑے تو اچھے سیتے ہو مگر دیر بہت لگاتے ہو۔ دو دن کا وعدہ کرتے ہو۔ آٹھ دن میں دیتے ہو۔

صاحب کیا کروں ؟ کام بہت ہے۔ سینے والے تھوڑے سے ہیں۔ اپنی طرف سے تو بڑی کوشش کرتا ہوں پر دیر ہو ہی جاتی ہے۔

107

کراچی

میں کل کراچی جاؤں گا اور وہاں ایک ہفتہ ٹھہروں گا۔ کراچی پاکستان کا سب سے بڑا شہر ہے۔ یہ بین الاقوامی ہوائی اڈا اور ایک معروف بندرگاہ ہے۔ میں ایک ہفتے کے قیام میں پہلے یونیورسٹی دیکھوں گا۔ یہاں کی لائبریری سے کچھ کتابیں حاصل کروں گا۔ پھر نیشنل میوزیم اور قومی عجائب خانہ میں کچھ نایاب چیزیں، بچوں کا۔ آخر میں کچھ دوستوں سے ملوں گا اور ان کے ساتھ چند تفریحی مقامات کی سیر کروں گا۔ امید ہے وہاں سے دو دوست میرے ساتھ لاہور آئیں گے۔ ان کی بیویاں بھی ساتھ ہوں گی۔ وہ سب چند روز لاہور میں قیام کریں گے اور وہاں کی تاریخی عمارتیں دیکھیں گے۔

اخبار کا مطالعہ

اخبار کے مطالعے سے ہمیں دنیا کے تمام اہم واقعات کی خبریں گھر بیٹھے مل جاتی ہیں حکومت کا کوئی نمائندہ، کوئی سیاسی لیڈر، کوئی مذہبی رہنما اگر کسی جلسے میں اپنے خیالات کا اظہار کرتا ہے تو اگلے ہی دن اس کی تقریر اور تصویر اخبار میں چھپ جاتی ہے۔

اس کے علاوہ اخبار میں اشتہار، مزاحیہ کالم اور ادارے بھی شائع ہوتے ہیں۔

موجودہ دور میں اخباری صنعت کافی ترقی کر چکی ہے۔ اب اخبارات صرف سیاسی خبریں نہیں دیتے بلکہ سیاسی خبروں کے ساتھ ساتھ مختلف موضوعات پر مضامین بھی شائع ہوتے ہیں۔ ایک ہفتے کے اخبارات کے کئی رنگین ایڈیشن بھی شائع ہوتے ہیں۔ ان میں عورتوں اور بچوں کے لئے الگ صفحات وقف ہوتے ہیں۔ پاکستان میں سب سے زیادہ اخبارات اردو میں چھپتے ہیں۔

ٹیلی ویژن

ٹیلی ویژن دورِ حاضر کی مقبول ترین ایجاد ہے ۔ اس کے موجد کا نام جان ایل برڈ ہے ۔ مغربی ممالک میں اس کو پچاس برس سے استعمال میں لایا جا رہا ہے ۔ پاکستان میں اس کا استعمال ۱۹۶۶ء سے شروع ہوا ۔ پہلے چند بڑے شہروں میں ٹی وی سٹیشن قائم کئے گئے ۔ اب سٹیشنوں کی تعداد زیادہ ہو گئی ہے اور پروگراموں کا دائرہ وسیع ہوتا جا رہا ہے ۔

ٹیلی ویژن کے ذریعے دنیا کے لوگ ایک دوسرے کو بہتر طور پر سمجھ سکتے ہیں ۔ کسی ملک کے سیاسی رہنما، دانشور اور حکمران اپنا نقطۂ نظر عوام کے سامنے پیش کر سکتے ہیں ۔

کار

میں نے ایک کار خرید رکھی ہے ۔ یہ کار سفید رنگ کی ہے ۔ اس کی قیمت دو لاکھ
روپے ہے ۔ صبح کو میں کار پر دفتر جاتا ہوں اور دوپہر کے بعد واپس آجاتا ہوں کار کو گیراج
میں کھڑا کر دیتا ہوں اور کام کے تمام دروازے اچھی طرح بند کر کے تالے لگا دیتا ہوں ۔
ابھی یہ کار دس ہزار میل چلی ہے ۔ یہ بڑی خاموش اور تیز رفتار کار ہے ۔
کار زیادہ تیز نہیں چلانی چاہیئے ورنہ قابو سے باہر ہو جاتی ہے اکثر حادثات تیز رفتاری
کے باعث ہوتے ہیں ہمیں کار چلاتے وقت ٹریفک کے قوانین کی سختی سے پابندی کرنی چاہیئے ۔

111

کوچوان

محلے کی گلی کے موڑ پر تین چار تانگے ہر وقت موجود رہتے ہیں مگر اس روز وہاں ایک بھی تانگا نہیں تھا ۔ مجھے خاصی معذ دور بھی جانا تھا اور جلدی بھی پہنچنا تھا اس لئے تانگے کا انتظار کرنے لگا ۔ تا نگے تو بہت سے گزرے مگر سب لگے ہوئے تھے ۔ اچانک میں نے فیکے کوچوان کو اپنی طرف آتے دیکھا تو پکارا بھئی فیکے تانگا کہاں ہے ؟ تا لگا لاؤنا ۔ " تانگا تو بابو جی آج نہیں جوڑا ہے۔" فیکے نے جواب دیا ۔ میں نے دیکھا کہ فیکے نے آج شیو نہیں بنوایا تھا اور ان کی آنکھیں بھی سرخ ہو رہی تھیں ۔

" کیا بات ہے ؟" میں نے پوچھا

وہ بولا : " آپ میرے بابو کو تو جانتے ہیں نا ! اس کی ایک آنکھ چلی گئی ہے ۔

" اوہو ، کیسے گئی ؟ کیا کوئی حادثہ ہوا ؟

انگلستان میں غیر ملکی

لندن میں ہزارہا یہودی روس سے آتے ہیں اور جلد ہی لاکھوں کا کاروبار کرنے لگتے ہیں ۔ چند سال کے بعد وہاں کی قومیت اختیار کر لیتے ہیں اور ان کی اولاد ہر اعتبار سے انگریز بن جاتی ہے ۔ فرانسیسی، جرمنی، ارمنی، یونانی، اطالوی، ہسپانوی اور پرتگالی غرض ہر ملک کے باشندے انگلستان میں روزی کما رہے ہیں ۔

اب انگلستان میں پاکستان کے باشندے بھی کثرت سے ہیں ان میں سے کچھ تو پڑھے لکھے ہیں مگر بیشتر ان پڑھ ہیں ۔ یہ لوگ کارخانوں اور دوکانوں میں محنت مزدوری کرتے ہیں اور جب کچھ رقم بچا لیتے ہیں تو پھر بیویوں بچوں کو بھی وہاں بلا کر رفتہ رفتہ مستقل طور پر وہیں آباد ہو جاتے ہیں ۔

دو بَیل

جانوروں میں گدھا سب سے بے وقوف ہوتا ہے اور گدھے کے بعد بیل ۔ کئی گاڑیوں میں ایک شخص جھوری کہتا انھا ۔ اس کے پاس دو بیل تھے ایک کا نام ہیرا تھا اور دوسرے کا نام موتی دونوں جسم کے مضبوط تھے دونوں میں محبت ہوگئی تھی ۔ وہ ایک مدرسے کے سامنے بیٹھ کر اشاروں میں بات چیت کرتے تھے ۔

ایک مرتبہ جھوری نے دونوں بیل چند دن کے لئے اپنے سسرال بھیجے ۔ وہاں پہنچ کر انھیں رسوں سے باندھ دیا گیا اور کھانے کو بھی کچھ نہ ملا ۔ آدھی رات کو دونوں نے زور لگا کر رسے تڑوا لئے اور اپنے گاؤں واپس پہنچ گئے ۔ صبح اٹھ کر جھوری نے دیکھا کہ دونوں لی دروازے پر کھڑے تھے اور دونوں کی گردنوں میں آدھا آدھا رسہ لٹک رہا تھا ۔

114

اصفہان کا تاجر

شاہ عباس کے زمانے میں ایک تاجر اصفہان میں رہتا تھا۔ تاجر کا نام حاجی قربان علی تھا۔ اس کے پاس روپیہ، جائیداد اور زمین بہت زیادہ تھی ۔ ہر شخص اس کو پہچانتا تھا ۔ اور جہاں بھی جاتا لوگ اس کو عزت واحترام سے دیکھتے ۔ اس شخص میں بھی یہ خوبی تھی کہ ہر شخص کو یکساں عزت اور احترام سے ملتا تھا اسے غریبوں سے نفرت نہیں تھی بلکہ دن رات کوشش کرتا تھا کہ ان کی حالت بہتر ہو جائے ۔

حاجی قربان علی محنتی ، دیانت دار اور فہمیں آدمی تھا وہ غریبوں کی مدد کرتا تھا ۔ انھیں کھانا کھلاتا تھا اور ان کی مالی مدد بھی کرتا تھا ۔

115

لطیفہ

ایک شخص نے کسی آدمی کو سڑک پر جاتے دیکھا ۔ وہ اس کے پیچھے تیزی سے گیا اور کہا
جناب! آپ کی طبیعت کیسی ہے؟ مدت سے آپ کو نہیں دیکھا ۔ آپ کمزور ہو گئے ہیں
آپ کے سر کے بال بھی سفید ہو گئے ہیں ۔ پرویز صاحب! یہ سب کچھ کیسے ہوا؟
اس آدمی نے جواب دیا ۔ جناب آپ کو غلط فہمی ہوئی ہے میں پرویز نہیں ہوں ۔
اس پر پہلا شخص بولا : کتنے افسوس کی بات ہے آپ کی ہر چیز بدل گئی ہے ۔ یہاں تک
کہ نام بھی بدل گیا ہے ۔ آپ کا نیا نام کیا ہے ۔
اس آدمی نے جواب دیا : عزیز ۔ میرا نام کبھی پرویز نہیں تھا ۔ آپ بھول گئے ہیں ۔
پہلے شخص نے جواب دیا : آپ کبھی بھول گئے ہیں میرا نام عزیز نہیں ہے ۔

لاہور کا جغرافیہ

لاہور پنجاب میں واقع ہے لیکن پنجاب اب پنج آب نہیں رہا۔ اس زمین میں اب عرف
چار دریا بہتے ہیں ۔ جو نصف دریا ہے وہ اب بہنے کے قابل نہیں رہا ۔
کہتے ہیں کسی زمانے میں لاہور کا حدود اربعہ بھی ہوا کرتا تھا ۔ لیکن اب لاہور کے چاروں
طرف بھی لاہور ہی واقع ہے ۔

لاہور کے لوگوں سے یہ خواہش کی ہے کہ دوسرے شہروں کی طرح ہمیں بھی آب و ہوا
دی جائے ۔ میونسپلٹی بڑی بحث و تمحیص کے بعد اس نتیجے پر پہنچی کہ اہل لاہور کی یہ خواہش
نا جائز نہیں لیکن بدقسمتی سے کمیٹی کے پاس ہوا کی قلت تھی اس لیے کمیٹی سے جا بجا دھوئیں
اور گرد و کے مرکز کمول دیئے ہیں جہاں یہ مرکب مفت تقسیم کئے جاتے ہیں ۔

کمیٹی نے کروڑوں روپے خرچ کر کے پانی کے نل لگوا دیئے ہیں فی الحال ان میں ہائیڈروجن
اور آکسیجن غیر ہے لیکن ٹھہرا ایک ایک دن یہ گیسیں ضرور مل کر پانی بن جائیں گی۔

آندھی

بہار کا موسم تھا ۔ مارچ کا مہینہ ابھی دو دِن سے پہلے نکلا ہوا تھا ۔ اٹھارہ میل دور ایک گاؤں میں پہنچنا تھا ۔ راستے کا منظر نہایت خوبصورت تھا ۔ دھوپ کسی قدر تیز تھی مگر ناگوار نہیں تھی ۔ ہوا میں بھینی بھینی خوشبو تھی ۔ آم کے درختوں میں بور آ گیا تھا ۔ جگہ جگہ کھیتوں میں کسان کام کر رہے تھے ۔ گنے اور جَو بوزے کے لئے فصل تیار ہو رہی تھی ۔ کسان ہل چلا رہے تھے میں گھوڑے پر سوار تھا اور سوچ رہا تھا کہ دو گھنٹوں میں گاؤں کے سامنے سے گزرنے والی پکی سٹرک پر پہنچ جاؤں گا ۔ اتنے میں آندھی آ گئی ۔ غبار اٹھا اور اندھیرا اس طرح پھیل گیا کہ سب منظر نظروں سے اوجھل ہو گیا ۔

مچھر

یہ بھنبھناتا ہوا اتنھا سا بھنگا آپ کو بہت ستاتا ہے۔ رات کی نیند حرام کردیتا ہے۔ ہندو، مسلمان، عیسائی، یہودی سب مچھر سے نالاں ہیں انسان طرح طرح کے مسلکے بناتا ہے کہ ان کو بوسے مچھر بھاگ جائے لیکن وہ اپنے حملے سے باز نہیں آتا۔ امیر، غریب، ادنیٰ و اعلیٰ، بچے بوڑھے کوئی اس کے وار سے محفوظ نہیں۔

مچھر کے کاٹنے سے ملیریا بخار ہوجاتا ہے۔ ملیریا ایک دن چھوڑ کر چڑھتا ہے۔ کچھ دنوں میں مریض کو بے حد کمزور کردیتا ہے۔ جب ملیرے کے انسداد کی دوائیں ایجاد نہیں ہوئی تھیں اس وقت یہ بہت تباہی مچاتا تھا۔ مگر اب کونین کی ایجاد سے یہ بخار خطرناک نہیں رہا۔

CONTENTS

PART I

Chapter   I   SCRIPT ....
Chapter   II   GRAMMAR ....
Chapter   III ....
Chapter   IV   TENSES ....
Chapter   V   ....

PART II

CONTENTS

PART I

Chapter I   SCRIPT 123

Chapter II   GRAMMAR 128

Chapter III   GENDERS AND NUMBERS 130

Chapter IV   TENSES 132

Chapter V   SOME MORE GRAMMAR 146

PART II

EXERCISES   148

Chapter I (refer to page 11)

SCRIPT

II
Urdu Alphabets

A complete mastery over the 'detached forms' of Urdu alphabet is necessary before the learner starts writing the 'joined forms' of the letters. Write the following letters from right to left:

ش ٹ ٹ ت پ ب

و ڈ ڈ ٹ د

ژ ز ز ڑ ر

ض ص ش س

ظ ط

ن ل گ ک ق ن

ہ

ی

Write the letters given below from left to right:

خ ح چ ج

غ ع

ے

123

Write the following two letters upside down:

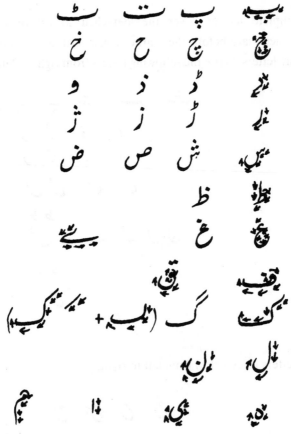

Move your pen in the direction of the arrows for writing various letters correctly and complete them by putting dots and other signs above or below each letter in the following manner:

III
Vowels

Twelve vowels are used in everyday Urdu conversation but only seven of them are committed to writing.

124

The long vowels, *i.e.*, ﺢ ، ﯽ ، ﻭ ، ﺍ are to be written as directed in the preceding section.

When " ﺢ ، ﯽ " is joined with other letters its shape is abbreviated and two dots are placed below it in the following manner:

Full Form	Abbreviated Form
ﯽ	ﻳ
ﺢ	ﻳ

The three short vowels are called zabar (◌َ), zēr (◌ِ) and pēsh (◌ُ). The horizontal line, in each case, indicates a letter. Zabar and pēsh are placed above the letter and zēr below it. Zēr (◌ِ) is placed below the letter '   ' like this: "   ". Similarly zabar and pēsh will be placed over the letter in the following manner:

Suppose the letter ' ﺑ ' is to be joined with the letter '   ', thus short vowels will be placed as given below:

Separate Form	Joined Form	Transliteration	
ن ﺑِ	ﺑِن	bin	
ن ﺑَ	ﺑَن	ban	
ن ﺑُ	ﺑُن	bun	

IV

It is desirable to practise writing Urdu alphabet according to the following shape-groups:

125

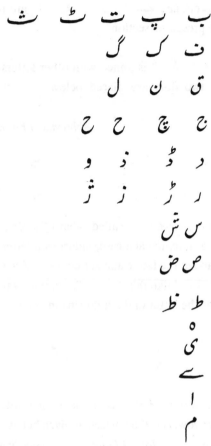

ب پ ت ٹ ث

ف ک گ

ق ن ل

ج چ ح خ

د ڈ ذ و

ر ڑ ز ژ

س ش

ص ض

ط ظ

ء

ہ

ے

ا

م

V
Consonants

A list of consonants (as well as vowels) has been reproduced above. Below is a list of aspirated consonants. They fall into four shape-groups and should be practised in the like manner:

126

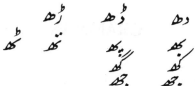

Move your pen in the direction of arrows for writing these consonants in the correct way:

First Step	*Second Step*	*Final Shape*

Note: Sections II to V of the book should be practised extensively and every detached letter written dozens of times before proceeding further.

VI

The section written in the original book is self explanatory and should be practised extensively, as instructed earlier.

VII, VIII, IX, X

All words of these sections should be written repeatedly for mastering the Urdu script.

Chapter II

GRAMMAR

EXERCISE 2 (page : 29)

1. This is my pen.
2. That is my book.
3. This is our office.
4. This is our shop.
5. Is that your house?
6. No, that is not my house.
7. This is his newspaper.
8. Is that our library?
9. Yes, that is our library.
10. It is your lock.

EXERCISE 3 (page : 29)

1. The book is on the table.
2. The man is in the room.
3. The water is in the glass.
4. The chair is in the house.
5. From the school to the house.
6. From Lahore to Karachi.

EXERCISE 4 (page : 29)

1. That is a post-office.
2. This is not a key, (it) is a lock.
3. This is a table, not a chair.
4. Is the book on the floor?
5. No sir, it is on the table.

6. Is it not a bedstead (chárpáee)?
7. No, it is a table.
8. The milk is cold.
9. The tea is hot.
10. The book is green and the pen is red.
11. The tree is big and the plant is small.
12. The girl is pretty and the boy is ugly.
13. (There) is a paper in my pocket.
14. (There) is a flower in my hand.
15. His shirt is new.
16. His pen is new.
17. Our house is far from the college.
18. What is your name.
19. This book is clean and that newspaper is dirty.
20. The knife is sharp and the table knife is blunt.
21. I am a student.
22. You are a gardener.
23. You are a teacher.
24. You are a little boy.
    (Thou art a little boy.)
25. We are in the garden.

Section X   (page : 31)

1. What is your name?
2. Who is in the house?
3. How are you?
4. Where are you now-a-days?
5. Why are the boys happy?
6. When is his examination?
   (When is his examination going to be held?)

Chapter III

GENDERS AND NUMBERS

I
I. Gender   (page : 32)

Masculine		Feminine	
1.	boy	9.	girl
2.	room	10.	stick
3.	door	11.	window
4.	glass	12.	cap
5.	dog	13.	street (lane)
6.	cloth	14.	chair
7.	horse	15.	mare
8.	he-goat	16.	she-goat

II. EXERCISE 1   (page : 36)

1. They are boys.
2. They are girls.
3. Where are the women?
4. The books are on the tables.
5. The chairs are in the rooms.
6. The women are in the homes.
7. Who are in the rooms?
8. The boys are in the school.
9. The cars are on the road.
10. The clothes are in the shops.

EXERCISE 2   (page : 36)

1. What is your name?
2. Who is the owner of the house?
3. The doors of the shop are beautiful

4. This is the book of that woman.

5. This is the shirt of the man.

6. The hair of the girl are black.

7. The light of the bulb is dim.

8. The minarets of the mosque are white.

9. The window-pane (pane of the window) is not clean.

10. The table-cloths (cloths of the tables) are dirty.

Chapter IV

TENSES

EXERCISE (English translation)

(page : 39)

1. (You) go to the school.
2. (You) read the book.
3. Write on the notebook.
4. (Please) come in the house.
5. (Please) send the servant to the shop.
6. (Please) put the book on the table.
7. (Please) sit in the chair.
8. Go immediately and bring (some) paper from the market (bazár).
9. Put the pen in your pocket.
10. Pour (some) sugar in the tea and shake it with the teaspoon.
11. Bring (some) fruit from the market (bazár).
12. (Please) drink cold water.
13. (Please) eat hot chapáti (cake of bread).
14. (Please) take the book and give it to your friend.
15. (Please) walk slowly.

EXERCISE (English translation of the Urdu sentences)

(page : 41)

1. Where did our car go?
2. I went to Lahore yesterday.
3. When did you come from the office?
4. The servant brought clothes from the tailor.
5. The boys went in the garden.
6. The girls came from the school.
7. The women brought cloth from the market.
8. You met your friend there.
9. We reached the station late.
10. I went to bed late tonight.

EXAMPLES IN SENTENCES   (page : 42)

English Translation of the Urdu Sentences

1. The teacher bought a pen.
2. The teacher read the book.
3. The girl saw a mare.
4. The girl saw a horse.
5. The woman read the book.
6. The woman read the book.
7. The boys learnt the lesson.
8. The doctor gave the medicine.
9. The doctor gave the medicines.
10. The dog ate the meat.
11. The dogs ate the meat.
12. You read the newspaper.

EXERCIES (page : 43)

Past Indefinite of Transitive Verb

English Translation of the Urdu Sentences

1. I read the magazine.
2. We read the books.
3. The servant drank tea.
4. The man saw the horses.
5. The women saw the horses.
6. I cut down the tree.
7. I cut down the trees.
8. Who opened the gate?
9. The thief took the watch out of my pocket.
10. You saw a snake.
11. You saw two snakes.
12. What did we buy from the market?
13. We bought a cap.
14. I wrote on the paper and you read (it).
15. The teacher told stories to the children.
16. The mother told a story to the child.
17. The father gave one rupee to his son.
18. The girl did not drink tea.
19. The girl did not drink water.
20. The man did not eat bread.

Past Perfect Tense

Translation of the examples at page 44

Past Indefinite	*Past Perfect*
1. I read the book.	I have read the book.
2. The servant cut the tree.	The servant has cut the tree.
3. Who opened the door?	Who has opened the door?

4.	Why did you write the letter?	Why have you written the letter?
5.	The teacher wore the cap.	The teacher has worn a cap.
6.	The washerman washed the clothes.	The washerman has washed the clothes.

Examples of the Past Perfect (Distant type).

	Past Indefinite Tense	*Past Perfect (Distant)*
1.	I read the book.	I had read the book.
2.	I read the books.	I had read the books.
3.	We sang a song.	We had sung a song.
4.	The shopkeeper sold the caps.	The shopkeeper had sold the caps.
5.	The cat drank milk.	The cat had drunk milk.
6.	The washerman washed the clothes.	The washerman had washed the clothes.

EXERCISE

Present Perfect (Near and Distant Past)

Translation of Urdu Sentences (page : 45)

1. The shopkeeper has gone to Karachi.
2. My friend had gone to Karachi last year.
3. I had not gone to the school yesterday.
4. The girl has gone to the college today.
5. The boy did not go to the college today.
6. When did you go to England? (had gone)
7. My brother has come from America.
8. The servant had come in the room and I had gone out.
9. The Police has caught a thief today.
10. The teacher has not taught the lesson today.

Compound Verbs   (page : 46)

Examples

(*a*) 1. The child got tired.
    2. The friend came. (did come)
    3. The servant finished his work.
    4. Did you read the lesson?
    5. Did he do my work?

(*b*) 1. Who has taken away our car?   (page : 47)
    2. I have come (back) from Karachi, now.
    3. The girl has bought a book.
    4. The woman has read the magazine.
    5. Have you dressed yourself?
        (Have you put on the clothes?)
    6. The washerman has washed the clothes.
    7. The servant has given my shirt to the washerman.
    8. The wife has put the utensils in the almira.
    9. We had opened the door.
    10. He had eaten the food and had gone out.

Examples: (page: 47)

    1. I have put on the coat.
    2. The girl has taken her meals.
    3. We have drunk water.
    4. You have delivered the speech.
    5. The women have left the city.

EXERCISE   (page : 48)

    1. The dog runs fast.
    2. The women eat meals.

136

3. At what time does the postman come here?
4. At what time do you come (back) from the office?
5. At what time does your daughter come back from the college?
6. The boys read from the books and write on the notebooks.
7. Do you play cricket now-a-days?
8. The girl does not play badminton.
9. I do not play football now-a-days.
10. My friend smokes cigarettes and I drink tea.
11. The woman eats rice and the man eats bread.
12. Why do you not understand me? (Why don't you get my point?)
13. Do you do business? (Are you a businessman?)
14. She still studies in a school.
15. The gardeners work in the gardens and their women (female family members) work in the houses

Present Continuous Tense

English translation of the illustrations at page 49

	Present Indefinite	*Present Continuous*
1.	I go.	I am going.
2.	We write letters.	We are writing letters.
3.	The women cook food.	The women are cooking food.
4.	You speak Urdu.	You are speaking Urdu.
5.	Where do you go?	Where are you going?
6.	The child eats toffee.	The child is eating toffee.

EXERCISE (page : 49)

1. He is working very hard.
2. The woman is boiling the milk.
3. You are washing your hands with soap.
4. We are playing cricket in the ground.
5. The girls are listening to an interesting story.
6. You are hiding something from me.
7. Are they still sleeping?
8. They are not sleeping, they are awake.
9. What are you saying?
10. I am not saying anything.

Past Imperfect (page : 50)

English translation of the sentences.

Present Imperfect (Indefinite)	*Past Imperfect (Indefinite)*
1. He goes to Lahore.	He used to go to Lahore. (He went to Lahore).
2. You sing the song.	You used to sing the song.
3. The boys read the books.	The boys used to read the books.
4. The girls read the books.	The girls used to read the books.
5. The girls sleep.	The girls used to sleep.

Past Imperfect Continuous (page : 50-51)

Present Imperfect (Continuous)	*Past Imperfect (Continuous)*
1. He is going to Lahore.	He was going to Lahore.
2. You are singing a song.	You were singing a song.

138

3. The girl is reading a book. The girls was reading a book.
4. The girls are sleeping. The girls were sleeping.

Perpetual Present and Past (page : 51)

English translation of the Urdu sentences

Perpetual Present Tense	*Perpetual Past Tense*
1. The boy goes. (The boy is in the habit of going)	The boy used to go.
2. He sleeps at noon.	He used to sleep at noon.
3. You sing.	You used to sing.
4. The girls play.	The girls used to play.
5. I take a walk everyday.	I used to take a walk everyday.
6. We take tea in the evening.	We used to take tea in the evening.
7. You eat rice at night.	You used to take rice at night.

Aorist Tense

Translation of the sentences at page 54

1. When you go to Islamabad, you must see Faisal Mosque.
2. If you get tired soon, take rest.
3. If you go to Karachi, you may forget Lahore.
4. When I reach New York, you please do see me.
5. If I study, I may pass the examination.

Future Tense (page : 55-56)

Exercise

1. My brother will sleep in the room.
2. There will be a great rush on the road tomorrow.

3. Will you come to Pakistan next year.
4. Walk slowly lest you fall on the wet floor.
5. We shall take a walk in the garden tomorrow.
6. The dog will run fast.
7. We shall drive the car all day long.
8. You will get up late tomorrow.
9. The cat will drink all the milk.
10. The women will go to sleep early tonight.
11. Will you not go to the office the day after tomorrow?
12. We shall not watch T.V. again.
13. The teacher will teach the lesson.
14. The shopkeeper will not open the shop tomorrow.
15. The college will remain closed tomorrow. It will re-open the day after tomorrow.

Conditional Future Tense

Translation of the sentences on page 56
1. If you come to my house, you will be benefited.
2. I shall get up when the sun rises.
3. If I eat too much, I shall get sick.
4. If you climb the ladder, you will fall.
5. When the gardener comes, he will cut down the tree.

EXERCISE (a)   (page : 57)

1. Your servant may be a thief.
2. My wife might be at home at the moment.
3. My friend might be in the office today.
4. You may not be there tomorrow.
5. They may be your brothers.

EXERCISE (b) (page : 57)

1. He may be going to the office everyday.
2. You might be preparing for the examination.
3. The girls might be taking a walk daily.
4. You might not be doing anything even now.
5. He may be meeting him last year as well.

EXERCISE (c) (page : 57)

1. You might have come here before.
2. I might have committed a mistake.
3. The women might have come from the market.
4. You might have gone to America.
5. You might have read this book before.

Use of Infinitives in Sentences
(a)

English translation of the examples on page 58

1. He will go home to get some sleep.
2. He went to Karachi to see his friend.
3. I am going there to play.

(b)

1. I am going there to play.
2. We are going there to see the match.
3. Will you go with me to take your meals.

(c)

1. It is goo to go to sleep and to rise early.
2. It is a bad habit to tell a lie.
3. It is my habit to read books.

141

4. It is a crime to give or take bribe.
5. Who does not know how to sing and cry?

Expressing two actions in quick succession

English translation of the Urdu sentences on page 59

1. I did not see anybody on (after) reaching there.
2. I got tired after along walk.
3. I felt pain in my belly after taking food.
4. What did you see on reaching there?
5. When I woke up the sun had risen.
6. I will take tea on reaching home.
7. Will you watch T.V. while lying down.
8. We shall play after taking tea.
9. You will not listen to the radio while lying down.
10. I shall take food while standing.

Direct and Indirect Speech

English translation of the examples on page 60

1. My friend said, "What is your full name?" (Direct)
   My friend asked what my full name was. (Indirect)
2. The teacher ordered the students,
   "Leave the class immediately." (Direct)
   The teacher ordered the students to
   leave the class immediately. (Indirect)

Passive Voice

English translation of the examples on page 61

1. I was shown books in the library.
2. The soldier was killed in the battle.
3. The officer was not seen in the office yesterday.
4. The poor man was served with meals.
5. Hard work is being taken from us.
6. His crying can not be borne by me.
7. Our team could not play well today.
8. You could not sleep peacefully at night.
9. It is my habit not to reply the letters early.
10. The tree shall be cut down because it has grown old.

Use of 'Sakná' and 'Saká'

English translation of the exercise on page 61 – 62

1. Women can learn languages easily.
2. You can go everywhere.
3. Nobody can stop me.
4. Everybody can go to see the match.
5. You cannot sit down.

English translation of the examples on page 62

1. I could not sleep last night.
2. You could not write a letter.
3. We could catch the bus yesterday.
   We caught the bus yesterday with difficulty.
4. Couldn't you eat meals today.
5. The boys could not play football today.

Action done under compulsion

English translation of the examples on page 62-63

1. I had to go to the office.
2. We had to eat rotten food.
3. You have to go to the college everyday.
4. One has to sleep when tired.
5. One has to study for the examination.
6. You will have to go to Karachi now.
7. Man will have to die one day.

Use of Chahná and Cháhiyē

English translation of the examples at page 63

1. We should work carefully.
2. We should learn Urdu.
3. You should read this book.
4. I should eat bread.
5. Everybody should work hard.

Past, Present and Future Forms of "Cháhná"

English translation of the examples given at page 63

1. I want to go to America.
2. Do you want to eat rice?
3. We want to sleep now.

4. Why did you like to go.
5. We wanted to sleep during the day.
6. I wanted to use the fan but it was out of order.
7. I would like to write a letter to my friend.
8. Would you like to take rest.
9. The girl would like to read the book.
10. The women would not like to play just now.

Chapter V

SOME MORE GRAMMAR

Degrees of Comparison

English translation of the 'examples' on page 64

1. My horse is better than your horse.
2. My elder son is more capable than the younger son.
3. The sister runs faster than the brother.
4. She is the most beautiful girl.
5. He is the most intelligent boy.

Use of 'Áp' and 'Apná'

Exercise at page 66

1. He is driving his own car.
2. You are polishing your shoe.
3. I am telling my story.
4. You are spoiling your watch.
5. The child is tearing his book.
6. The father is beating his son.
7. You are not doing your work.
8. The boy is memorizing his lesson.
9. The girl is washing her face.
10. The teacher.is putting on his coat.

Use of 'Sá'

English translation of the examples on page 67

1. Please bring some tea.
2. There are many papers lying on the table.
3. Please drink some milk.

Examples

1. There is no one like you.
2. Every one saw the rose-like face of the girl.

Part II

EXERCISES

Introduction (Refer to page : 82)

[*A person whose name is Rashid, has come from Karachi. He goes to an office at Lahore where he wants to see an officer whose name is Yousaf*]

Rashid: (To the office peon) Is Mr. Yousaf in his office?

Reon: Yes sir.

Rashid: Please give my (visiting) card to him.

[*Peon goes in with the card and comes back after a while*]

Peon: Mr. Yousaf is waiting for you. Please go in.

[*Rashid enters (the room)*]

Rashid: (To Mr. Yousaf) Assalámo álakum (Peace be on you).

Yousaf: Wá álakmus salám (and peace on you also).

Rashid: My name is Rashid and I have come from Karachi. I am working in a 'Company' there.

Yousaf: What can I do for you?

Rashid: My company has sent me to you on an official business.

[*Rashid tells him the details of the matter*]

Yousaf: It will be done within a few days.

Rashid: I am thankful to you. Now I beg leave. May God protect you.

Yousaf: May God protect you.

148

Travel by a Train   (page : 83)

Passenger:	(To the taxi driver) I want to go to the railway station.
Driver:	Right sir, I shall do it.
Passenger:	How far is the station from this place?
Driver:	It is not too far, it is only 6 km.
Passenger:	(After reaching the station) Where is the ticket window?
Driver:	It is right in front.
Passenger:	(At the ticket window) Please give me a ticket for Multan.
B. Clerk:	In which class do you want to travel?
Passenger:	Air conditioned. How much does it cost?
B. Clerk:	Two hundred rupees.
Passenger:	(At the enquiry window) Is the train for Multan late?
Clerk:	No sir, it is right in time.
Passenger:	How much time does it take to reach Multan?
Clerk:	Five hours.

Air Travel   (page : 84)

Passenger:	Do you have a seat for America.
Clerk:	When do you want to leave?
Passenger:	I want to leave on the 3rd of March.
Clerk:	A flight leaves on the 3rd of March at 5 P.M.
Passenger:	Right. Give me a ticket.
Clerk:	Do you want one way ticket or return ticket?
Passenger:	One way.
Clerk:	Do you smoke.
Passenger:	No sir. Give me a window seat.
Clerk:	Right sir. (you will get it.)
Waiter:	(To the passenger) Would you like to have some drink sir?

149

Passenger:	What can I have?
Waiter:	Lemon, Coca-Cola, tea, coffee.
Passenger:	Coffee will do.
Waiter:	Right sir.
Passenger:	What time would the plane leave and what time would it land at New York airport?
Waiter:	The plane is going to take off within few minutes and would reach New York in eighteen hours.

In the City   (page : 85)

Passenger:	(To the taxi driver) Take me to some middle class hotel.
Driver:	Right sir, please be seated in the taxi.
Passenger:	What fare would you charge?
Driver:	According to the meter, at rupees 3 per km.
Passenger:	(To the receptionist at the hotel) I want a bedroom.
Receptionist:	Room No.310 situated on third floor is vacant.
Passenger:	(To the waiter) Please carry the luggage upstairs.
	[*After taking rest, the passenger wants to have a look at the city*]
Passenger:	(To the receptionist) I want to go sightseeing. Can you get me a taxi?
Receptionist:	Why not. The hotel has its own taxi service. Where would you like to go?
Passenger:	I want to visit Rawal Dam first. From there I shall go to Islamabad and would like to see Faisal Mosque.
Receptionist:	I'll call the driver and instruct him.
Passenger:	Right, Thank you.

Dialogue I   (page : 86)

Mr. Rahim: Doctor! My daughter is not well.

Doctor: Ask your daughter to lie on this bed.

Mr. Rahim: She has been unwell since yesterday

Doctor: What did she eat yesterday?

Mr. Rahim: Yesterday we were invited to a function. Perhaps she ate something bad, there.

Doctor: Does she have pain in the belly also?

Mr. Rahim: Yes sir.

Doctor: Do not worry. I have examined her thoroughly. Here is a prescription. Get the medicines from the market. Give her two tablets with water every four hours. She will be alright by tomorrow.

Dialogue II   (page : 87)

Doctor: Madam! Don't worry. I have examined him thoroughly. Exhaustion is the cause of fever. Perhaps your husband has over-worked these days.

Wife: I have told him scores of time not to work so hard lest he loses his health, but to no avail.

Doctor: I have properly instructed him to take a complete rest the whole day.

Wife: What are the timings for giving the medicine?

Doctor: Medicine is not required. Make sure that he takes rest. There should be no noise in the patient's room.

Wife: Don't worry.

[Doctor goes]

Wife: (To the husband) I say . . . Are you sleeping?

Husband: I was just lying quietly.

Wife: Doctor has strictly forbidden you to talk.

151

Husband:	Hooṅ. [Just a nasal sound]
Wife:	Do you feel much pain?
Husband:	Hooṅ.
Wife:	What will you take? Orange juice, soup or sago with milk.
Husband:	Orange juice.
Wife:	It will not do, take soup, it gives strength.

Pakistan (page : 88)

Pakistan came into existence on August 14, 1947. Now Pakistan consists of four provinces and its population is approximately ten crores (hundred millions). Population-wise the Punjab is the biggest province, followed by Sind and North-West Frontier Province. Baluchistan has the least population, although area-wise it is the biggest province. All the four provinces of Pakistan are very important in their own right. Wheat, rice, cotton, sugarcane and maize are the chief crops of the Punjab and Sind, from which Pakistan earns valuable foreign exchange apart from meeting its domestic needs. Karachi is the biggest city of Pakistan which is situated in Sind. It is a big industrial and commercial centre, an international airport and a natural seaport. Most part of the Frontier Province is mountainous. Its biggest city is Peshawar. Baluchistan is rich in minerals. Big deposits of natural gas have been discovered at 'Sui' a village in Baluchistan, which is used as fuel throughout Pakistan.

The World Map (page : 89)

Pakistan is situated in the continent of Asia, France is in the European continent and Egypt in the African continent.

If you have a look at the world map, the north is upwards and the south downwards. The east is on the right side and the west on the left.

China is situated in the northern side of Pakistan and India in the south as well as the east. Iran is in the west. Afghanistan is in the north-west. The sun rises in the east and sets in the west. Pole-star is always in the north. The big oceans are situated to the south of the world.

Seasons   (page : 90)

Pakistan has four major seasons; the winter, the spring, the summer and the rainy season. The summer is the longest season. Temperature starts increasing in the month of April and goes on rising continuously till the month of July. The rainy season starts in the middle of July and continues for two months. When this ends, the winter sets in. We experience severe cold in the months of December and January. Weather starts changing again in the month of February. This is the beginning of the spring season. The flowers start blooming everywhere. People begin strolling in the gardens. The fragrance of flowers spreads everywhere. This season comes to an end in April and again the long summer starts.

Fruits of Pakistan   (page : 91)

Many fruits grow in Pakistan. Fruit is good for health. Amongst the fruits in Pakistan, banana, orange, kino, mango, apple, guava and grapes are liked more. The mango is very sweet and delicious. Apple is good for health. Now the production of orange and kino has increased manifold in Pakistan.

Dry fruit is liked in winter. Peanuts, chilghozá (*Pinus gerardiana*), walnuts and almonds are dry fruits. Dry fruit is costly in Pakistan but the other fruit is cheap.

The Post Office (page : 92)

Post offices are found in every town and village in Pakistan. We buy envelops and stamps from the post office. Money orders are also distributed through the post office.

After writing a letter, we drop it in a red letter box. The postman opens this box at a fixed time and takes away all letters in a bag. In this way, all letters are collected in the general post office of the city where they are sorted and despatched to various places either by train or by air.

Urgent messages are sent through telegram.

Lahore (page : 93)

Lahore is a big city of Pakistan. It is an old and historical city. It was inhabited centuries ago. It is situated on the bank of River Ravi. Lahore is the capital of the Punjab. All the offices of the provincial government are situated here. The city has been the capital of the province since long. Different Kings built many buildings and parks here. People come to visit these places from far and wide.

In Lahore, the places worth visiting are the museum, the zoo, Jinnah garden, the Shalimar garden, Minar-i-Pakistan, Badshahi mosque, and Iqbal's mausoleum.

A Village School (page : 94)

I study in a high school situated at a distance from my village. I live in the school-hostel. Forty boys from various villages reside in this hostel. A teacher has been appointed to supervise the activities of the students of the hostel.

When the call for morning prayer is heard, all the boys get up. They take ablution and say prayers. Some of the boys go for a walk. After some time, all the boys gather in a big room and take breakfast. After breakfast they change their clothes, prepare their bags and go to the school. The school building is adjacent to the hostel.

In the school, teaching continues till noon. When the school closes, the students again come back to the hostel. After lunch they take rest for some time. After that some boys go to the school playground to play football. Again, in the evening, they dine together and then the time for the studies begins.

Importance of Playing (page : 95)

One must spare some time to play. It brings joy and the body becomes active. Look! the boys are playing in the ground. They jump and run as they like. They are playing cricket. One boy is very active but the other seems lazy. One boy falls down while running but he is not hurt. Therefore, in a short while, he will again get up and start running.

Playing is very important but it is not good to play all the day long. The boys who play all the time are unable to learn their lesson and fail to pass the examination.

The Knife (page : 96)

Look at my knife! It is made of steel. I bought it for ten rupees. I cut fruit with it. It is very sharp. Do not move your finger on it. You may cut your finger. Do not throw it into water. It might get rusted. It can be dangerous to hand over the knife to a child. Fruit is peeled with the knife and vegetables are prepared (for cooking). If you cut wood or something hard with the knife, it will become blunt.

The Pets   (page : 97)

The dog, the cat and the hen are pet animals. They are found throughout the world. The dog is a faithful animal. It loves its master and also protects the house. The cat lives inside the house. It is fond of milk. it is an enemy of the rats. The rats run away when they see it approaching.

The hen lays eggs. We also eat its flesh. Now many poultry forms are being developed in Pakistan. The flesh and eggs of the hen are tasty and full of energy.

The Cow and the Buffalo   (page : 98)

The cow gives milk. The buffalo also gives milk. People are fond of drinking the milk of the cow and the buffalo. The she camel, the goat and the sheep also give milk but their milk is not tasty. The milk of the buffalo is thick and tasty. The milk of the cow is yellowish. The buffalo is usually black and sometimes brown. The cow has various colours.

The butter, the cooking oil and the yogurt is prepared with milk. Many sweet meats are also prepared with milk.

Some Useful Animals   (page : 99)

The horse, the ox, the donkey and the camel are useful animals. They are used to carry load. They are also yoked to the plough or the cart. In Pakistan, oxen are also yoked to the plough.

The horse is used for riding. It is also used for pulling the cart and carrying load. The donkey is a poor animal by nature. It can live with the poorest food available. It carries all types of load. The camel is known as the ship of the desert. It is only the camel which can walk on the sand while carrying load.

The man domesticated these animals, thousands of years ago and has used them for he progress of the world eversince.

Some Etiquettes of Eating   (page : 100)

There are some peculiar etiquettes of eating. They should be taken care of. before taking meals one should wash one's hands and face. One should eat small bits of food. One should be careful that the curry does not stain the clothes. Food should be properly chewed before being swallowed. A little less food should be eaten than the actual desire. Over eating must be avoided. Eating in a hurry is harmful. Food should be chewed slowly with teeth so that no sound is produced while eating. After meals one should wash one's hands and clean one's teeth once again.

The Mother and the Daughter   (page : 101)

Fauzia's mother is cooking food in the kitchen. When the meals are ready, all members of the family will sit together and eat. Little Fauzia is sitting in the adjoining room. She has a pencil in her hand. A thick sheet of paper is lying on the table. She is drawing a picture on the sheet with a pencil.

The mother came from the kitchen and enquired from Fauzia what she was doing. She replied that she was drawing the picture of the fruit basket on the paper.

Look! how cleverly the bananas, the oranges, the apples and the mangoes have been drawn. Various colours have also been filled so that the drawing looks like real fruits.

The Sun   (page : 102)

When the sun rises, the darkness disappears. The light spread everywhere. People get busy in various jobs.

Look! someone is going to the office, another is going to the factory. Children are going to their schools. Had there been no sun, there would have been no life. Because of the heat of the sun, flowers bloom plants grow and fruits ripe on the trees. The wheat, the rice and other crops also ripe because of the heat. The sun rays kill the germs of the diseases. It is pleasant to sit in the sun during winter.

The Death of the Soldier   (page : 103)

The brave soldier was carried from the battlefield to the hospital. Every part of his body had been wounded. One hand had been blown off by the cannon ball. The lower part of the right leg was also missing. The left eye had also gone. Apprehending that he was about to die an urgent telegram was sent to his wife. The unfortunate woman reached the hospital, the next day. Hearing the news of the death of her husband, she screamed and fell unconscious.

Urdu in Pakistan   (page : 104)

You can learn Urdu within a short time. Urdu is the national language of Pakistan. It brings people of various parts of the country together. Therefore, you can easily move about throughout Pakistan if you learn Urdu. Last year a foreigner, who did not know Urdu, came to Pakistan. He could not see the country to his desire. He stayed in the northern areas for a few days but because of the language problem could not visit the remote areas. Therefore, all foreigners should learn Urdu before going to Pakistan.

The Dress (page : 105)

We wear dress to cover our body. In Pakistan, men wear pants and coats or shalwar and kameez. In the villages, many people tie a chadar (sheet of cloth) round their waist in place of shalwar. Kurta (Tunic) is also worn instead of a shirt. It is a loose dress which is good for summer.

We wear woollen dress in winter and light dress in summer. In addition to the woollen and cotton clothes, dress made of nylon is also much in fashion now-a-days.

The Washerman (page : 106)

The washerman is washing the clothes. Look! it is high noon now but he is till standing in the knee deep water. His son is sitting nearby. His wife has brought food from home. When he finishes his work, he will move out of the water and take his meals under the shade of some tree. An ox is standing near him and a dog is keeping watch.

Now, in big cities, this job is not much profitable. The laundry and dry cleaning shops are in abundance where the clothes are washed with the help of big machines. Many clothes are thrown into a machine. When the machine works, the detergent removes the dirt from the clothes. Clean and dry clothes come out of the machine. After ironing they are packed.

The Tailor (page: 107)

The tailor is sewing the clothes. This tailor is a very skillful man. He cuts and sews the cloth in such a way that it admirably fits the body. That is why he is so famous. There is a

159

heap of pieces of cloth lying in his shop. He also has many apprentices.

Look! the apprentices are sewing the clothes and the tailor, with a scissors in his hand, is cutting the cloth. Iron is lying nearby. When the clothes are ready, the customers try them on.

Master! you stitch the clothes very well but deliver them after a long time. You promise to prepare them within two days but you actually take eight days.

Sir, what can I do. Work is heavy, workers are few. I try my level best yet it gets late.

Karachi   (page : 108)

I shall go to Karachi tomorrow and stay there for one week. Karachi is the biggest city of Pakistan. It is an international airport and a busy seaport.

During my stay, I shall visit the university first. I shall get a few books from its library. Then I shall sell certain rare things to the national museum. Lastly, I shall see some friends and visit a few recreation spots with them. I hope two friends will accompany me to Lahore. They will stay at Lahore for a few days and shall see places of historical interest.

The Newspaper Reading   (page : 109)

By reading newspapers, we get the news of the important events of the world by sitting at our homes. When some government official, political or religious, expresses his views in a public meeting, his speech and photograph is published in the newspapers next day.

In addition to the news, there are advertisements, light reading columns and editorials in the newspapers.

The newspaper industry has made a lot of progress during the present age. Newspapers not only give news but also print valuable articles on current affairs.

The newspapers also publish a few colour editions in a week. Special supplements are published for women and children. In Pakistan Urdu newspapers have the largest circulation.

Television (page : 110)

Television is the most popular invention of modern times. The name of its inventor is John L. Bird. It has been in use in the Western world for fifty years. In Pakistan, it started in 1965. First of all T.V. stations were established in a few big cities. Now they have grown in number and the area receiving the telecast has also increased.

The people of the world can understand one another better through T.V. Political leaders, intellectuals and representatives of the government can present their points of view through T.V.

The Car (page : 111)

I have purchased a car. Its colour is white. Its price is two lacks (one hundred thousand rupees). In the morning, I go to my office in the car and return home in the afternoon. I park it in the garage and lock all the doors. It has done ten thousand miles so far. It runs fast and does not produce any noise. We should not drive the car very fast otherwise it would go out of control. Most of the accidents take place because of over speeding. We should strictly observe the traffic rules while driving.

The Coachman (page : 112)

We always find three or four tongas standing on the turning of the lane of the locality. But on that particular day, no tonga was to be found there. I had to go quite some distance and was in a hurry. Therefore, I stood there, waiting for a tonga. Many tongas passed by but all were booked. Suddenly I saw the coachman 'Feeka' coming towards me. I shouted, "oh, where is your tonga? Bring it for me."

"I have not got it ready today," Feeka replied. I noticed that Feeka had not shaved today and also his eyes were red.

"What is the matter?" I said.

He replied, "You know my father. He has lost one eye."

"Very sad, how did it happen? Was it some accident?"

Foreigners in England (page : 113)

Thousands of Jews come to London from Russia and soon settle down in business worth millions. After a few years they get the English nationality and their children become Englishmen in every sense of the word. French, German, Armenian, Greeks, Italians, Spaniards and Portuguese, in short the people of every country, are earning their livelihood in England.

Now Pakistani nationals are also found in large numbers. Some of them are educated but most of them are illiterate. They work in factories and shops and when they have saved enough money, they arragne for the migration of their wives and children. Gradually they settle down permanently.

Two Oxen   (page : 114)

The donkey is the most foolish of all animals followed by the ox. A person named jhoori lived in a village. He had a pair of oxen which were called Heera and Moti. Both were strong in body. Both loved on another. They talked making signs to one another while sitting.

One day jhoori sent the oxen to his in-laws for a few days. There they were tied with ropes and also got nothing to eat. At the dead of night they broke the ropes applying power and returned to their village. In the morning, jhoori saw that both of them were standing on the door of his house and broken ropes were hanging by their necks.

The Trader of Isfahan   (page : 115)

During reign of king Abbass a trader lived in the (city of) Isfahan. His name was Haji Qurban Ali. He had a lot of money, estate and land. Everybody knew him. Wherever he went, people respected him. He had the quality to meet everybody with equal respect and reverence. He did not hate the poor, on the contrary he tried to improve their lot, day and night.

Haji Qurban Ali was hardworking, honest and intelligent. He helped the poor, provided them food to eat and also gave them financial help.

A Joke   (page : 116)

A man saw some one going on the road side. He ran after him and said, "Sir, How do you do? I have not seen you for a long time. You have grown weak. Your hair has also turned grey. Mr. Parvez! how did all this happen?"

The man replied, "You are mistaken, I am not Parvez."

At this the first man said, "How sad! you are completely changed. You have changed even changed your name."

The man replied! "My Dear (Aziz) My name was never Pervez You have also forgotten. My name is no Aziz (Dear).

The Climate of Lahore   (page : 117)

Lahore is situated in the Punjab but Punjab no longer has five rivers. Only four and a half rivers flow in the Punjab now. The remaining half of the river does not flow.

It is said that Lahore was surrounded on all four sides by other places but now it is Lahore all around.

The people of Lahore demanded that they should be provided with water and air like the other cities. The municipal committee, after long discussions, came to the conclusion that this demand was not unjustified but unfortunately the 'committee' did not have enough water and air, therefore, it opened a few centres of dust and smoke here and there, which are now distributed free of cost.

For water supply, the committee has spent millions of rupees on water pipes and hydrogen and oxygen has been filled in them. One day these gases will surely change into water by coming into contact with one another.

A Village Scene (page : 118)

It was spring season and the month of March. I was on an official tour. I had to reach a village at a distance of eighteen miles. It was a beautiful sight. The sun was a little hot but not intolerable. There was a sweet fragrance in the air. The mango trees were laden with small buds. The farmers were working in the fields here and there. The fields were being prepared for sugarcane and melons. The farmers were ploughing. I was on horse back, thinking that I shall be able to reach the road in front of my village within two hours.

Suddenly came a dust storm. Dust rose up and darkness spread in such a way that the entire scene was lost to eyesight.

The Mosquito   (page: 119)

This small buzzing insect bothers you very much. It deprives you of sleep at night. The Hindus, the Muslims, the Christians and the Jews are all unhappy with him. We prepare a lot of mixtures to drive the mosquito away with their odour but it persists in attack. The rich, the poor, the low, the high, the children and the old are its victims. None is safe against its attack.

The Malaria fever is caused by mosquito bite. The temperature of the patient rises on alternate days. The patient becomes very weak within a few days. It caused great destruction when anti-malaria medicines had not been discovered but now with the preparation of quinine, it is no longer dangerous.